WHAT HAPPENS IN THERAPY

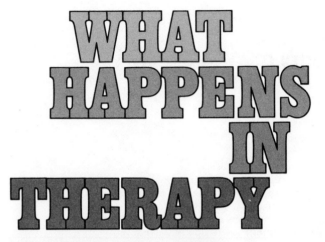

WHAT HAPPENS IN THERAPY

by SARA GILBERT

WITH A FOREWORD BY DR. BERTRAM SLAFF,
Director, Adolescent Psychiatry Clinical Service,
The Mount Sinai Medical Center, New York City

LOTHROP, LEE & SHEPARD BOOKS
NEW YORK

COPYRIGHT © 1982 BY SARA GILBERT
ALL RIGHTS RESERVED. NO PART OF THIS BOOK MAY BE
REPRODUCED OR UTILIZED IN ANY FORM OR BY ANY MEANS,
ELECTRONIC OR MECHANICAL, INCLUDING PHOTOCOPYING,
RECORDING OR BY ANY INFORMATION STORAGE AND RE-
TRIEVAL SYSTEM, WITHOUT PERMISSION IN WRITING FROM
THE PUBLISHER. INQUIRIES SHOULD BE ADDRESSED TO
LOTHROP, LEE & SHEPARD BOOKS, A DIVISION OF
WILLIAM MORROW & COMPANY, INC., 105 MADISON
AVENUE, NEW YORK, NEW YORK 10016.
PRINTED IN THE UNITED STATES OF AMERICA.
FIRST EDITION
1 2 3 4 5 6 7 8 9 10

LIBRARY OF CONGRESS CATALOGING IN PUBLICATION DATA

GILBERT, SARA D.
    WHAT HAPPENS IN THERAPY.

    BIBLIOGRAPHY: P.
    INCLUDES INDEX.
    SUMMARY: A LOOK AT ADOLESCENT THERAPY: WHAT
IT IS, WHY IT'S NEEDED, WHAT'S INVOLVED IN THE
FIVE MAJOR TYPES OF TREATMENT, AND HOW TO
MEASURE SUCCESS.
    1. PSYCHOTHERAPY—JUVENILE LITERATURE. I. TITLE.
RC480.G5   616.89'14   82-15233
ISBN 0-688-01458-5 (LIB. BDG.)   AACR2
ISBN 0-688-01459-3 (PBK.)

For Virginia David Lucey,
with thanks—for the idea
and for all the rest (so far!)

AUTHOR'S NOTE

I would like to express my deep gratitude to the following psychiatrists, psychologists, and social workers for their information, guidance, and ideas, which contributed greatly to this book: Ted E. Becker, M.D.; Gary Brill of the Peninsula Counseling Center in Woodmere, New York; Shelley Doctors, M.D., of the Montefiore Hospital (New York) adolescent unit; Laurie Gilkes, C.S.W.; Raelene Gold, M.D.; Linda Kestenbaum, Ph.D.; Richard Oberfield, M.D., of the Bellevue Hospital (New York) adolescent psychiatric unit; Ingrid Rozé of The Door, A Center of Alternatives, in New York City; Richard Rutkin, Ph.D.; Richard Wortman, M.D., of the Mount Sinai Hospital (New York) adolescent unit. And special thanks to Dr. Bertram Slaff.

Please note that the cases presented here are examples only; although they are typical of teenage problems and therapies, they are not based upon actual people. More important, they are not case studies shared by any of the above-mentioned therapists, who fully protected their clients' confidentiality while providing insights and direction for this book.

CONTENTS

FOREWORD

In *What Happens in Therapy* Sara Gilbert has accepted
a formidable challenge: how to communicate to teenagers, troubled or untroubled, the reality of the
therapeutic process. She has avoided the peril of
writing an overly complete, textbook-like compen-
dium on the one hand, and on the other hand has
managed to escape the pitfalls of oversimplification
and professional jargon. She understands well the
qualities of teenage confusions and uncertainties
and offers real help to young people trying to decide
whether they, or someone they know, may need professional assistance and how to proceed if the answer is yes.

As director of the adolescent psychiatry clinical
service at The Mount Sinai Medical Center in New
York City, I see a number of disturbed young people

11

who may be depressed and suicidal, or who may be
having a psychotic break, or who may be in an extremely difficult family situation. In my private practice I work with a number of teenagers who are
distressed to a somewhat lesser degree. Although
these individuals may seem to be suffering less, their
need for help may be just as great.

Unfortunately, the people who might benefit
most from therapy are often the least likely to be
aware of it. Obviously keen to this, Ms. Gilbert describes mild symptoms of trouble for which some
form of psychotherapy might be useful. She also
describes severe symptoms for which a person
should receive immediate help. Her judgments are
very sound, and she is wise enough to mention various stress points during adolescence, including
painful big successes as well as troublesome major
disappointments.

I can illustrate from my own experience an example of success as a stress. One summer I worked
intensively with a "golden boy," who had been selected as valedictorian of his high school class. He
was the president of his class, captain of the baseball
team, and had been voted "most likely to succeed."
He had been awarded an all-expense scholarship to
the university that was his first choice. To all this he
had reacted with despondency and increasing anxiety about his ability to maintain this level of achievement. As a result, he was even considering
abandoning the idea of college.

During our sessions it became clear that his parents had long been aware that they had a highly gifted child. To forestall his becoming conceited about his advantages, they had told him frequently that he was the inheritor of excellent genes that enabled him to be healthy, athletic, attractive, and academically at the head of his class. Unfortunately, he had read into this that he could not claim any credit or gratification for his achievements, that they were simply an expression of his genetic inheritance. However, if he were to fail at college, or in any other area of his life, this would clearly be his fault. It had become a no-win situation, and he was strongly tempted to "want out."

Therapy helped this young man understand his parents' overemphasis on genetics and how he had lost sight of the possibility of gaining satisfaction from his own efforts. Gradually, he began to experience himself more as a person, rather than as a carrier of superior genes. His despondency began to lift, and he finally resolved to embark on his college career.

Ms. Gilbert includes examples of other such troubled teenagers to illuminate a variety of treatment approaches, as well as complex psychological concepts such as conscious and unconscious, thinking and feeling, conflict, and transference. Her selection of adolescent problems is representative of those I see in my practice, and the range of therapeutic strategies discussed is comprehensive. *What*

Happens in Therapy should be extremely helpful to young people—whether they are weighing therapy for themselves or someone else, affected by a friend's or family member's treatment, or just curious about the process—their parents, and concerned youth professionals.

> Bertram Slaff, M.D.
> Director, Adolescent Psychiatry
>   Clinical Service, The Mount
>   Sinai Medical Center,
>   New York City
> Past President, American Society
>   for Adolescent Psychiatry

WHAT HAPPENS IN THERAPY

1
THERAPY: WHAT IT IS AND WHAT IT ISN'T

Janet, who was fifteen, felt as though she had been "miserable forever." It seemed to her that she had no friends. She hated the way she looked and acted. Besides, nothing she did seemed to work out right.

Janet wished that she could go into psychotherapy, or therapy as it is commonly called, because she thought it might help her feel better. At the very least, a therapist might be able to say what was *wrong* with her. But what if it turned out that a lot was wrong? That thought frightened Janet. She also wasn't sure she wanted to get involved in the long and complicated process she thought therapy would mean. And she had no idea how to go about finding a therapist. She didn't even know how to talk to her parents about it; she was sure they wouldn't want to pay the high cost, especially because only crazy peo-

17

ple went to therapists—and they'd tell her she wasn't crazy.

◆ ◆ ◆ ◆

Janet had a lot of mistaken ideas about psychotherapy, as many people—adults as well as teens and children—do. This book will clear up many of those mixed-up impressions and common fears by describing how therapy works, what it can and cannot do, and the various reasons for which young people may want or need to turn to therapy for help.

You will learn first of all that psychotherapy, especially for young people, is often not "long and complicated"—or necessarily expensive. You will also find out that therapists—whether psychiatrists, psychologists, psychoanalysts, social workers, or some other professional—rarely *tell* people what is "wrong" with them. Rather, they help people come to a better understanding of themselves, by themselves.

Another common misconception is that only people who are mentally ill go to psychotherapists, so being in therapy—"having your head shrunk"—*proves* that you have serious mental problems. You will discover that this is far from true. Not only can therapy help deal with lots of situations besides "craziness," but seeking help from a therapist (or allowing therapy to help) can also be a sign of strength and health. Just as much of a physician's job is to keep people healthy, rather than simply to cure disease, much of psychotherapy is devoted to helping basically well people sort things out, resolve daily conflicts, and feel better about themselves. It also gives people a resource that they can turn to throughout their lives when problems arise.

WHY NOT?

Okay, so if therapy can be so useful, why does it make people uncomfortable and often ashamed to talk, or even to think, about it? Here are some of the arguments against therapy that you may have heard.

"The therapist will find out that something's wrong with me." We all have thoughts, dreams, wishes, feelings, or memories that we consider strange—sometimes so strange that we're afraid to mention them to anyone. Teenagers may think they have many such "dark secrets" to hide, because adolescence brings with it many new and confusing experiences. Much of Janet's "misery," in fact, stemmed from natural teenage confusion.

Therapists, though, have seen this kind of "normal craziness" in many people of *all* ages. Rather than finding out that there's something wrong with you, a therapist can help you see either that some of your dark secrets really aren't so unusual, or that they have causes that are easily explained.

"The doctor will take control over me." Many people believe that therapists can read minds. If they can *read* minds, such thinking goes, they can control minds: through a kind of brainwashing or with drugs or hypnotism they can make someone do, feel, and think what *they* want. The term *headshrinker,* or *shrink,* to mean "therapist" came about because of this fear of being controlled or losing control. Headshrinkers in primitive societies were witch doctors who could perform magic (as in "read minds") and who removed the brain from a victim's skull.

Naturally, this kind of thinking can make people afraid of psychotherapy. But the facts are:

1. Few therapists are hypnotists. Hypnotism may be useful in certain very unusual cases, but even under those circumstances no one can be hypnotized against his or her will.

2. Although responsible therapists of all sorts do recommend the use of drugs for a few specific situations, most are extremely wary of prescribing chemicals for teenagers. (Even then it's important to remember that no one can force you to take a drug, either!)

3. The most skilled and experienced thera-

pist cannot help someone who will not be helped. This means that if you go into therapy, the outcome depends mainly upon you. Nothing will happen unless you and the therapist enter into a partnership. Rather than controlling you, therapy should help you gain more control over your own life by making you more self-aware and more understanding of your potential.

"I'm okay!" If everything, truthfully, is going well for you, you have no need for psychotherapy. But if you are having problems in any two of these major areas of your life—

> school or work
> family life
> friendships or social relationships

—you can use some help. Janet, for example, sensed trouble in all of these key aspects. Also, *physical* discomfort for which a physican can find no cause may be a sign that you are not "okay"; emotional conflict often creates physical symptoms.

"I don't want to go!" Most (but not all) adults begin some form of psychotherapy because they choose to. They seek it because they want to understand themselves better, or because they have some problem that they can no longer handle alone. Most (but

not all) teenagers first meet a therapist because someone else—a parent, a school official, or a legal authority—has said that they *must*. (Janet will go on her own, but even so, she is reluctant.)

Few of us like to be forced into anything against our will, and teenagers often like it even less, resenting anything adults order them to do. But as one therapist who treats adolescents comments, "I point out to young people that by *not* doing something just because the adults in their lives recommend it, they are just as much under adult control as if they obeyed those adults blindly."

"Who needs an expensive listener?" One image that young people have gotten from popular media is that psychotherapists are like either pals or parents. "I can talk with my folks or my friends about this," they say, "so what's the point of paying money to talk?"

Well, for one thing, not all therapy is expensive; on pages 129-130 you'll find suggestions for sources that are free or nearly so. A more important reason, though, is that a therapist is someone who is *not* a member of your family or a friend, but someone who has enough distance from your past or present life to be able to see it more clearly. From this unique position, a therapist can help you see things more clearly, too. Even people who can understand and accept this difference may still feel that talking with a trained professional won't do any good. This is probably because they don't fully understand how therapy works.

THERAPY IS . . .

The word *therapy* literally means "treatment." Psychotherapy is different, however, from other kinds of physical or medical treatments. Though you must cooperate with a physical therapist by doing the right exercises, or with a physician or medical therapist by accepting prescribed treatment, in psychotherapy you must cooperate to a much greater extent.

You must still rely on someone else's expertise in psychotherapy, but you work less for a "cure" than for an understanding of yourself and your problems. This understanding may help resolve a current crisis and may become a tool for preventing future problems as well.

Imagine that you want to hang a favorite poster on the wall of your room. You know about nails and hammers, you think, but you can't put it all together —you can't make the nails stay in, and you keep hitting your thumb. You ask for help from someone who is more expert in carpentry than you and are told that you'll have much better luck if, instead of holding the hammer near the head, you grasp it at the end of the handle. Also, you learn that you're using the wrong kind of nail for the wall.

When you try it the new way, it works. You've had expert guidance, but *you* had to use the hammer. Have you "cured" your sore thumb? No—but you understand why you hit it, you've learned how not to do it again, *and* you've learned a constructive skill.

THERAPISTS DO . . .

In psychotherapy the "experts" may be psychiatrists, psychoanalysts, psychologists, social workers, or other types of therapists. Their job is not to solve problems for you, but to guide you toward your own constructive solutions.

There are probably many people in your life who are guides. Your parents may give you guidance, in the form of both advice and rules, about how to conduct yourself. Your teachers, coaches, or counselors can tell you how to get good grades, make the team, or get a job or a scholarship. Your friends can make suggestions about how to dress or get dates, and they can listen to your gripes about your parents and all your other guides. But no matter how many guides a person has, a therapist is different.

One definition of a therapist is "a skilled, professional friend." A good therapist is not a pal or a parent. She or he is on your side, will support you, will not judge or punish you for any of your thoughts or feelings—but has no reason to accept, love, or approve of you automatically in the way that family or friends usually feel they must.

Your pals and parents may (or may not) listen to you. A good therapist will listen to you in a different way. He or she should be able to "hear" what you don't say as well as what you do say, and to comprehend the feelings that you don't even know how to describe.

Therapists are also taught how to observe and interpret behavior as well as words. Through education or other training, they learn about a wide variety of human characteristics, about danger signals and healthy symptoms, and about comparing one person's words, thoughts, and actions with what people in general say, think, and do.

They are *not* taught, necessarily, to sit at the head of a couch on which a patient is lying and to say nothing but "uh-huh"! This image is a popular view of the therapeutic techniques developed by Sigmund Freud, the first "psychoanalyst," that appears often in books, movies, and cartoons about therapy. In fact, therapists of any kind who deal with teenagers, individually or in a group, almost always do so face to face; couches are rarely involved. Most say a lot more than "uh-huh"; they ask questions, respond, and offer support, advice, and enthusiasm when they are needed.

A good therapist may ask you questions that no one else has ever asked you—that, in fact, you may never have thought of asking yourself. If answering those questions makes you nervous or ashamed, just remember that whatever you say won't shock or go any further than your therapist.

You can tell your best friend a secret, but it may not stay private. The adults in your life may respond badly when you reveal something important about yourself; they may punish you or not take you seriously. We'll go into this matter of confidentiality more in later chapters, but for now you need to know only that, within some very broad limits, what you say to a therapist remains as secret as if you hadn't said it at all.

A good therapist is not interested in using you or changing you in the same way that others you deal with may want to. A therapist is interested in helping you understand (and perhaps change and make better use of) yourself. The simplest way of summarizing how this happens is this: in therapy you learn to connect feelings with behavior.

2
A LOOK BENEATH
THE SURFACE

"Therapy helps connect feelings with behavior? I already know how to do that!" you might protest.

You know that you slam the door of your room when you feel angry. You know that you feel good when you've gone out of your way to look good. You know that when you are in a bad mood you act rotten to everyone. You know that when you've tried to make someone else happy you feel happy, too.

That's good. Some people don't understand or believe that emotions are tied to actions. Perhaps because emotions are invisible, and actions are obvious to the senses, it doesn't seem possible that they can be related.

Take Peter, for example. At fourteen, he was sent to a psychiatrist by the juvenile court because he had been getting into a series of increasingly serious scrapes, at first with the officials at school, and then with the law. He had been told all his life that he was "bad." He was used to being punished by parents and teachers, but not to being "treated." It had never occurred to him that his angry behavior might have something to do with anger he felt inside. Therapy will help him understand why he might feel angry and how his behavior expresses that anger.

Peter's anger and treatment will be described in depth in Chapter 5. For now, think for a moment about how your own emotions and behavior might be connected. For instance, have you ever gotten into such an emotional fight—or started giggling so hard—with a friend that by the time you were done, you couldn't remember what started it all? Actions and feelings can form complex chains: one emotion triggers some behavior, which triggers emotion, which triggers behavior, and so on. . . . If some of these "chains" get tangled with others, or with the reactions of other people, expert help may be required to unknot them.

When you think about the countless feelings and actions you experience, alone or with a huge variety of people in many different situations, even in a single day, you can begin to understand how these connections might get tricky. Multiply them by all the days of your life (including those you think you can't remember), and it's clear that the process of "untangling" can be pretty complicated.

THE SCIENCE OF UNDERSTANDING

Humans are probably the only creatures who try to understand their feelings and behavior. What we have learned about ourselves forms the basis of a branch of science called psychology. *Psychology* literally means "study of the psyche." *Psyche* (pronounced "sigh-key") is an ancient Greek word for "breath" or "soul." Today it is used to mean the whole of the mind and personality—that special combination of thinking, feeling, and sensing that makes a person a person. Even though psychologists and other scientists have not yet been able to dissect or explain the psyche, they have agreed upon some of its characteristics.

They have discovered, for example, that there is one part of our thoughts, feelings, and senses of which we are aware; they label this the "conscious mind." And they have learned that there is another part of which people, no matter how "smart" they are, are unaware; they label this the "unconscious mind."

Your conscious mind is the part that "takes care

of business"; it runs your daily activities. If you have a test on Friday, your conscious mind tells you that you should study on Thursday. If your friend is nasty to you, your conscious mind tells you to stay away or to fight back. Your conscious mind holds onto the memories that you can easily recall: the best birthday party you ever had, the worst vacation you ever lived through, and the like.

Your *un*conscious mind, though, has at least as much control over feelings and behavior. It's the part that stores the experiences and impressions you might never be able to remember, and so it triggers the kinds of reactions that you "just can't explain."

The unconscious also protects the conscious from painful thoughts, keeping them hidden but not inactive. Psychologists have also found that feelings never totally disappear. No matter how deeply they are buried, they will come out in one way or another, including physical symptoms such as insomnia, headaches, or stomachaches. Unconscious thoughts and feelings may also be expressed in dreams, which have been called "the royal road to the unconscious." While we sleep, our mind relaxes, and many of the experiences that it has tied down may be released for a time. Even so, they may not yet be untangled, which is why, for example, a dream may seem to be "about" a friend or your grandmother's house, when what is really on your mind is yourself or school.

Although some types of therapy ignore dreams (and most don't follow rigidly the formal rules Freud developed for the interpretation of dreams), many therapists feel that dreams can offer clues to help explain otherwise "mysterious" thoughts or actions. Guided by a trained therapist, you may be able to discover the true meaning of your dreams and what that meaning says about you. Many people find, when working with a therapist who is interested in dreams, that they dream or recall their dreams a lot more than usual. If you don't dream or don't remember your dreams at all, this may be of interest to the therapist too. Actual absence of dreams can be a problem in itself. Lack of memory of dreams may mean a strong defense against an especially painful subject at the core of the unconscious.

The unconscious may also influence mistakes, accidents, and self-defeating behavior. If competition pressures you to make good grades, for instance, but you often manage to "forget" your homework, your unconscious may be behind a protest against the pressure. Or if you say you want to get your driver's license, but can't quite manage to pass the test no matter how much you practice, you may not be ready, unconsciously, for the responsibility of driving a car. A therapist may help you understand these kinds of behavior by exploring with you a part of yourself with which you were previously unfamiliar.

THERAPY'S BEGINNINGS

Many people simply do not believe that there are aspects of themselves that respond without their awareness. The "unconscious mind" and all the other theories of psychology just seem silly to them. It is true that these *are* just theories; no one can prove their existence.

But for centuries it has been observed that people behave in ways that cannot be explained rationally or sensibly. Once, strange behavior was blamed on demons or on unhealthy substances in the blood. "Haunting" by ghosts or spirits was one way of talking about the activities of what we now call the "unconscious mind." Later, doctors blamed "diseases of the nerves," which is what the word *neuroses* (or singular, *neurosis*) literally means. In the nineteenth century, nerve specialists attempted to treat what therapists do today.

In the early twentieth century, an Austrian doctor, Sigmund Freud, developed the concepts of the conscious and the unconscious mind as well as many other theories. Although many therapists who came after him quibbled with the details of his work, and more recent theories differ strongly with ideas that early followers of Freud accepted as fact, his psychoanalytic theories laid the groundwork for much of modern psychotherapy. Virtually all forms of therapy, for example, operate on the principle that there is *some* force beyond our immediate control that affects our behavior, our feelings, or both, although different groups may call it something besides the "unconscious" and locate it elsewhere than in the "psyche."

The same is true for many other Freudian concepts, such as the "ego," the "superego," and the "id." Freud divided the psyche into those three parts, which in very broad terms refer respectively to a person's outward personality, conscience, and primary physical and emotional needs. Today, many psychological theories shy away from those terms, but it is hard to find one approach that does not consider people to be some kind of three-part package, no matter what labels—"body, mind, and soul" or "physiological, intellectual, and spiritual"—are attached.

Various psychotherapies stress different aspects of this "package" more heavily than others. Some consider the physical more important than the mental, for instance; others place more importance on the conscious than on the unconscious. In general, though, all the methods have in common the belief that when one part conflicts with another, or gets tangled in difficult knots, problems arise in a person's life.

3
WHICH ONE?

Different types of therapy go about untying those "knots" in different ways. The broad group called "insight therapies" can be said to work from the inside out, connecting inner or past experiences to present actions and problems. "Behaviorist" therapists in general work from the other direction, altering behavior or solving immediate problems as a way of resolving inner conflicts. Some systems, like family therapy, crisis intervention, and residential treatment, combine various approaches.

It's important to have some information about the theories and procedures of both types and their variations in order to understand which one makes more sense for a particular person or problem and to have a feeling for what to expect from each. It is

34

not necessary, however—and in fact it can be undesirable—to be an "expert" in these matters before
treatment begins. As the old saying goes, a little bit
of knowledge can be a dangerous thing. One therapist puts it this way: "There's nothing worse than
meeting a patient who announces at the first session that he or she has fifty dreams to tell me
about."

INSIGHT THERAPIES

Insight therapy is sometimes called "analytically
oriented" because it analyzes, or dissects, a psyche
in order to understand it. It is concerned mainly
with the underlying causes of behavior, with the
unconscious sources of feelings and actions, on the
theory that once emotions and buried memories are
out in the open, they can't so easily trigger disturb-
ing behavior. It operates on the belief that if you can
understand those emotions and early experiences,
you can make changes within yourself.

Freudian psychoanalysis is the classic form of insight therapy. It relies on the patient's recalling and
linking a series of thoughts, memories, and feelings
("free association"), with little or no intervention
from the analyst, to make behavior understandable.
Many therapists have modified Freud's techniques
into less formal, less psychoanalytically oriented or

"neo-Freudian" methods. These are based on Freudian concepts, but the therapist provides more guided conversation. Some of these post-Freudian adaptations have, in turn, evolved precise theories and systems, or "schools of thought," of their own, which are usually named after their creators. Perhaps the best known of these are Adlerian therapy (after Alfred Adler), Jungian analysis (after Carl Jung), and Rogerian therapy (after Carl Rogers).

Insight therapies tend to use only conversation (although Jungians employ art and physical movement as well) and to focus on the relationship between the patient and the therapist. For Freud, one of the most important parts of the therapeutic relationship was "transference." By this he meant that patients apply or transfer to therapists the same range of emotions they direct toward the most significant people in their lives. Many neo-Freudians still believe that the emotional relationship between patient and therapist mirrors crucial "outside" relationships and that by working out and acting out those feelings, patients can better understand them and themselves.

"Insight" techniques are sometimes used to help people find the causes for their depression, for instance, or for a more general dissatisfaction with life. As we shall see in the case of Peter in Chapter 5, this form of therapy is also useful when the problem is an inability to get along with others. Insight-style therapy can also be beneficial for those who simply want to increase their self-understanding.

BEHAVIORIST THERAPIES

The approach that has been given the broad label of "behavior-oriented" deals primarily with present behavior and feelings. It tries to change what *is* without bothering too much about what *was,* on the theory that when behavior is changed for the better, what caused it will improve, too.

Formal "behaviorists" like Ivan Pavlov and B. F. Skinner learned that animals could be trained or "conditioned" to respond in certain ways when desirable actions were rewarded (as with food) and undesirable ones punished (as with electric shock). This conditioning process underlies all behavior-modification therapies, which use a variety of techniques to retrain people so that they can better control and direct their feelings and actions.

Behavior-oriented therapy tends to require fewer sessions than the insight approaches, and the therapist plays a much more active role. It may be suitable for the solution of particular, obvious problems, like addictions and phobias (irrational fears); we shall see in Chapter 6 how it helped Janet, whose difficulties stemmed more from her actions than from tightly tied internal "knots."

COMBINATION APPROACHES

Many of the more recent schools (today there are close to two hundred and fifty different therapeutic techniques) combine the insight and behaviorist approaches, or discard them completely in favor of a totally new theory.

The various activities of the "human potential" movement are examples of the melting-pot approaches. Through such techniques as "psychodrama" (role-playing), meditation, body movement, or highly structured group participation, human-potential advocates seek to help people "actualize" themselves in "body, mind, and spirit." Some of these groups, whose primary aim is self-awareness rather than the solution of particular problems, are developing into solid therapeutic schools; others are just fads.

Many of the group therapies that have been practiced long enough to have proven track records combine traditional and new techniques to provide ways of resolving a variety of problems. In self-help groups, for instance, participants who share a common trouble such as alcoholism, divorce, or obesity join together, with or without a trained leader, to give each other advice and support.

Family therapy is another combination approach, often utilizing group, individual, insight, and behaviorist techniques. When thirteen-year-old Alec, for instance, began having trouble getting along at home and at school, his parents thought there was something wrong with him. It quickly became apparent, though, that the whole family was going through a difficult period. The therapist in Alec's case, as we shall see in Chapter 7, worked with the entire family to resolve his problems and theirs.

"Crisis intervention" is yet another therapeutic method that uses a variety of techniques. In situations like Theresa's, described in Chapter 8, therapists practice a sort of "psychological first aid." Their goal is to help people gain insight into their feelings during a personal emergency while guiding them toward behavior that enables them to cope with the crisis at hand.

A different form of "crisis intervention" is used to rescue severely disturbed people, like sixteen-year-old Daniel in Chapter 9, whose mental illness required residential treatment. Patients with such serious disorders may also need follow-up treatment (often in hospitals or special therapeutic residences), which combines insight, behaviorist, individual, and group work with specialized medical care to help them understand and control their disease.

WHO DOES IT?

Any one of these forms of therapy can be practiced by people with a variety of backgrounds and training, including sometimes virtually no training at all. So for someone who is bewildered by the number of professionals to choose from, it is helpful to know what different titles mean.

A *psychiatrist* trains first to be a physician. After receiving an M.D. ("medical doctor") degree, he or she takes special courses to learn how to treat people's psyches. Although some physicians—body doctors—practice psychotherapy without this extra study, and any M.D. can prescribe drugs that affect the mind more than the body, a psychiatrist has special training in both areas. Psychiatrists, by the way, are the only therapists who are allowed to prescribe or administer medication.

A *psychoanalyst* (or *analyst*) is usually someone who has learned and practices the specific theories and techniques of psychoanalysis as set down by Sigmund Freud and his followers (or sometimes by lesser-known theorists). But psychoanalysts may come from a variety of backgrounds; they may be physicians, psychologists, or social workers, or they may be people without other related training who have decided to become analysts. Although many psychoanalysts are among the best-educated therapists, having passed through the rigorous training (which must include their own personal analysis) provided by recognized analytic institutes, it remains true that almost anyone may use the title.

Social workers make up the greatest percentage of psychotherapists. All of them have received social-work training at the graduate-school level (to receive the M.S.W. degree). And most (but not all) of those who serve as therapists have concentrated their studies in subjects related to psychology, psychiatry, or psychoanalysis. Social workers may hold jobs with private or public agencies, such as hospitals or clinics, or they may set up private counseling practices.

Psychologists do not hold an M.D. degree like psychiatrists. Like some social workers, they may have taken a variety of courses during college, though they may have majored in psychology. After college comes a master's degree (M.A.) and usually a doctorate (Ph.D.) in psychology. In addition, most psychologists who choose to work as therapists (rather than as researchers, for instance) train for about a year under the supervision of a practicing psychologist. This supervised work allows them to become "clinical psychologists," a title that differentiates them from psychologists who do laboratory or other research.

Most states require that psychiatrists, social work-

THERAPISTS AT A GLANCE

TITLE	REQUIRED TRAINING	REGULATIONS
Psychiatrist	College, M.D. degree, and three years of supervised residency	State license required, plus possible certification by American Board of Psychiatry and Neurology
Psychoanalyst	None required for practice, although professional associations may have requirements. Reliable psychoanalysts are doctors or social workers with years of extra study in an analytic institute	None
Social worker	College, two years of graduate school, supervised practice for Master of Social Work (M.S.W.) degree or more advanced work for Doctor of Social Work (D.S.W.) degree	Certification required by most states, also by Academy of Certified Social Workers for C.S.W. title

PROFESSIONAL ASSOCIATIONS	COMMENTS
American Academy of Child Psychiatry, American Medical Association, American Orthopsychiatric Association, American Psychiatric Association, American Society for Adolescent Psychiatry, psychotherapeutic or psychoanalytic societies	—Only therapist allowed to prescribe medication —Can follow any theory of psychotherapy —Some may tend to overstress the physical aspects; study at a psychotherapy institute may offset this
American Academy of Psychoanalysis, American Psychoanalytic Association, other psychoanalytic societies and institutes	—Though most analysts are Freudian, they may follow any theory of insight psychotherapy —Advanced degree (M.D., Ph.D., M.S.W.) and training in psychoanalytic institute indications of reliability
National Association of Social Workers; Academy of Certified Social Workers; psychotherapeutic and psychoanalytic societies	—Majority of therapists are social workers —Social workers may specialize in variety of work, so special training in therapy is good sign —Social worker therapists are usually less expensive than psychiatrists or psychologists

THERAPISTS AT A GLANCE

TITLE	REQUIRED TRAINING	REGULATIONS
Psychologist	College, four years of graduate school, one year of supervised training in psychology for Ph.D. degree. Clinical psychologists receive special therapeutic training	License or certification required in most states
Lay therapists: therapist, psycho-therapist, analyst, counselor, family counselor, marriage counselor	None. Anyone, trained or untrained, may use these labels	None.

ers, and psychologists obtain an official license to practice. The best of these therapists as well as psychoanalysts also receive certificates from the professional organizations that regulate them (see the chart on pages 42-45). Such certification means that therapists have received the training that their particular "school" says is necessary for them to prac-

PROFESSIONAL ASSOCIATIONS	COMMENTS
American Psychological Association; psychotherapeutic or psychoanalytic societies	—Can follow any theory of psychotherapy —Some psychologists have lesser degrees than Ph.D., so *may* not be as well trained —Psychologists may specialize in testing or laboratory research; clinical psychologists with training at therapeutic institutes are best as therapists —Usually cost less than psychiatrists
American Psychiatric Association, American Psychological Association, American Association for Marriage and Family Therapy, American Association of Marriage Counselors, and others *only* for those qualified	—Some untrained therapists are sensitive and helpful, especially for informal counseling —Degrees and training offer client more protection

tice, and that they conduct themselves within the ethical rules established by that group.

Any of the four therapists just described can practice any of the therapeutic techniques discussed earlier in this chapter—it all depends on the sort of training he or she has chosen. Any of them may work on a one-to-one basis with a "client" or "patient" (different schools use different names), may lead a group, or may combine individual sessions with group activities.

Also, it often happens that two or more of these experts work together. For instance, when Daniel suffered his sudden and severe mental and emotional collapse, he was helped back to health by the combined efforts of medical doctors, psychologists who gave him tests, psychiatrists who treated him, and social workers who assisted him and his family in adjusting to the crisis.

Finally, there are *lay therapists,* people without advanced degrees in medicine, social work, or psychology who have some sort of therapeutic training—or who have no training at all. It is possible, in fact, for anyone to set up a practice as a "therapist." Some of these people, even those without advanced degrees or officially recognized training, can be quite effective at helping people. (This is perhaps especially true in the case of the leaders of such self-help groups as Alcoholics Anonymous who have lived through the problem themselves and so have good ideas about how to aid others.) But some laypeople are simply fakes. In states that require proof of a therapist's competence before issuing a license to practice, these quacks may get around the law by calling themselves something other than "therapist." Through their lack of knowledge, experience, and sensitivity, incompetent therapists can do a lot more harm, besides cheating clients out of a bundle of money, than good.

HOW TO CHOOSE?

As you can see, there are so many varieties of psychotherapies and therapists that it can be hard to choose among them. So how do you find a therapist who is right for you? You may not be making the choice yourself, of course—your parents or some other adult may do the selecting—but you may still have a say.

The best way is to get advice and recommendations from people you trust, including the professional "helping people" in your life. Ask your doctor, your guidance counselor, and your religious leader, for example. Ask your friends about any experiences they've had with therapy. Call the local mental-health society; contact professional organizations of psychiatrists, social workers, or psychologists (see pages 128-129); or ask for recommendations at the adolescent or psychiatric unit of a large hospital. Is cost a problem? Find out about mental-health clinics in your area (some may be connected to a hospital; some may not). Teen centers or youth organizations may provide therapy or may be able to direct you to free or inexpensive help. Social-service organizations like the Chil-

HOW TO CHOOSE A THERAPIST

Factors to look for:

> Referral or recommendation by a friend or relative whom you trust, by a doctor or other professional, or by a recognized organization or helping agency (see pages 128-130)
>
> License or certification by the state, a professional body, or both
>
> Full membership in a recognized society or association for his or her specialty
>
> A postgraduate degree in the specialty, plus evidence of additional, supervised training
>
> An ability to make you feel comfortable
>
> A willingness to answer fully any questions concerning training, credentials, or therapeutic techniques

---

dren's Aid Society and those attached to religious groups also often offer psychiatric help.

In general, you're better off sticking with a professional, someone who is certified or licensed to practice psychotherapy. Although a degree or certifi-

Questions to ask:

> "What experience have you had in working with people my age?"
>
> "What experience have you had in dealing with my kind of problem, worry, or situation?"
>
> "About how long do you think therapy will take?"
>
> "How often would you want me to come?"
>
> "How much will it cost? Can extended payments or a sliding-fee scale be arranged?"
>
> "Are your services eligible for insurance coverage?"
>
> "What therapeutic theory or school do you follow?"
>
> "How will the process work? Individually? In a group? By talking only, or with other activities?"
>
> "Is there any reading on the topic I can or should do?"
>
> "How much will my parents be involved?"
>
> "Can I get in touch with you between sessions?"

cation is no guarantee that a professional will actually do you any good, you are at least protected by the state or the certifying organization if a therapist does you any harm. Also, many insurance policies that cover psychotherapy will pay only for treatment by a licensed professional. If you visit a clinic run by a mental-health society or some other social-service agency, you may be treated by people who are still in training or by laypeople, but they probably practice under the supervision of a professional on the staff of the organization.

Try to find, or ask for, a therapist who has had experience working with teenagers. Adolescent therapy has different requirements from therapy for children or adults, whose feelings and thought processes are not the same as teens'. Someone with little or no experience dealing with people your age will probably not be of much help to you.

You should meet with a therapist at least once before seriously beginning treatment. In this first session you (with or without your parents) can begin to feel comfortable with the situation. You should ask some basic questions, which a good therapist should be more than willing to answer fully. For example, you will want to discuss the kind of arrangements—time and money—that will be involved. How often will you have sessions, for instance? How much will everything cost? Is there a sliding scale to adjust fees to income? Will your parents' insurance cover some of the expense? Can they arrange an extended-payment plan?

You may be able to do all this yourself, especially if you seek counseling through a community clinic or teen center. But it is more likely, even when you enter therapy voluntarily, that your parents' participation will be necessary in some way. In some states therapists may not legally treat a person under a certain age without parental permission, although clinics often find ways to help troubled young people even when it is not strictly within the law. (The organizations listed on page 127 can explain your locality's specific laws.) Even where it is legal, many therapists will not deal with a teen whose parents have not agreed to treatment. In some cases, frankly, it is because they fear they will not get paid, but in most it is because their therapeutic technique requires at least some parental involvement.

In the end, all of this care in selection on your part will pay off. Your therapy will never get off the ground if the therapist you choose is ill suited to your problem—and to *you*.

4
WHY NOW?

For many reasons, adolescence is a likely time for therapy. This is because the eight to ten years it takes to pass from childhood to adulthood can be trying and upsetting.

Even teens in the most stable and contented families go through so many changes, so fast, that they may become confused and may even think that they are "going crazy." Parents are often going through a period of confusion of their own around the time their children become difficult, rebellious semi-adults. When these transition times collide, tensions are understandable. Professional help may be needed to ease them.

This is not to say that *all* teenagers, with or without their parents, need therapy! But many teens have questions about their bodies, their thoughts, or their feelings that they can't or don't want to discuss with their parents. And often parents can use outside advice on how to help their children through the sometimes troublesome pathway to adulthood. An expert can frequently help.

The teen years can be especially trying because they are, for many people, the first time *real* trouble occurs. You may be under new and heavy pressure, for instance, from your parents and your teachers to do well "now that it counts," and from your friends to act in a certain way or risk being left out. You may feel trapped in the middle or pulled in two or more directions at once, and either can create a lot of stress. Perhaps therapy of some sort could help you decide what *you* want.

During this period, too, you may experience more family trouble than you've been aware of before. Parents may be encountering more tension from work, finances, or personal problems than ever before, or perhaps it's the first time you've noticed these anxieties. When Theresa was thirteen, for example, her grandmother died and her parents divorced—which made a move necessary and strained the family finances. She felt, as many teens do, that she was "old enough to take care of herself," but she needed help to cope with all that change and loss.

What personal loss have you endured during the last year or so? Have you found somebody with whom you can share *all* your thoughts and feelings about that loss? A therapist can be that "somebody."

Also, now that you are a teenager, you can, probably for the first time, *get into* "real" trouble. Earlier we met Peter, whose problems had shifted from school and family hassles to conflicts with the law. Other familiar adolescent crises that might lead to psychotherapy are drug or alcohol abuse, sexual overactivity, or physical and emotional overreactions to tension. Not only do these cause serious problems, but, equally important, they are often the symptoms of some inner conflict that can be resolved by professional attention.

Finally, adolescence is also the time, according to psychological experts, when young people may be working hard to clear away all the pain and conflict of earlier years (frequently things that they weren't even aware of then) in preparation for assuming adult roles. That unconscious struggle may result in the uprooting of feelings and problems that were buried long before, and the resurfacing of old problems may complicate new ones. If confused young people get professional help right away in "digging up" their past, they may have less trouble in the future.

WHO NEEDS THERAPY?

As you can see, there are lots of good reasons that a teenager might want to turn to therapy. But how does a person know if he or she really *needs* it?

Someone like Peter, who got into serious—or increasingly serious—scrapes, was, at his young age, probably not a "criminal" but a troubled person. The "symptoms" of his trouble were petty crime, vandalism, and skipping school. But a kid with a heavy drug or drinking habit, say, or a pattern of violent reactions to minor events, is likely also to be showing signs of inner conflicts. It is important to know what those conflicts are—*why* a person does what he or she does. And it is important to know *now*, before the problems get too tangled or the trouble gets too deep.

A person like Janet, who wondered if therapy could make her less "miserable," probably would benefit from at least a few sessions with a professional counselor. She was not happy with herself or with her life—and it *is* possible to be happy. Again, it was important for her to know why, underneath, she was unhappy.

Sometimes people do not even know that they are unhappy, overly tense, in a state of emotional conflict, or even out of touch with reality. When we are in those situations, however, ·they always make themselves known through some activity of our bodies or our minds. Someone may, for instance, have trouble sleeping (whether in falling asleep, in waking up much too early in the morning, or in having upsetting dreams and nightmares) for more than a couple of weeks. Problems with food—eating far too much or far too little over a period of time

SYMPTOMS OF TROUBLE

Mild: A person could benefit from some form of psychotherapy who:

- has some trouble sleeping for more than a week or two
- has frequent headaches, stomachaches, or other fairly minor aches and pains for which there is no physical explanation
- has unexpected trouble with schoolwork
- feels uncomfortable with other people or has unusual problems getting along with others
- tends to overreact to events with too-strong anger or sadness
- is "tired all the time"
- goes at top speed all the time
- feels a frequent need for drugs of any sort
- is involved in an unusually large number of petty problems or minor "accidents"
- feels constantly hungry and gains weight rapidly, or is "never hungry" and loses weight fast

A person should seek help especially, but not only, if one or more of these symptoms closely follows one of the stress points listed on page 59, or if a combination of two or more of them persists for more than a couple of weeks.

Severe: A person should receive *immediate* psychological help who:

- feels worthless and hopeless most of the time
- has frequent thoughts or daydreams about self-destruction
- has frequent thoughts or daydreams about harming others
- has trouble getting one particular idea, fear, or fantasy off his or her mind
- has such fear of anything (such as small places, large crowds, germs, heights) that it interferes with daily life
- sees things or hears voices that other people cannot see or hear
- shows sudden, sharp changes in personality, behavior, habits, or mood
- responds with inappropriate emotions, such as laughing at sad news or crying at happy news
- often appears unable to carry on a conversation that makes sense—changing topics in mid-sentence, for instance, or giving an answer unrelated to the question asked
- suffers severe headaches or other pain that has no physical cause
- suffers severe, persistent insomnia and/or nightmares
- is involved in more than the usual number of serious accidents, conflicts, or illnesses
- is convinced of having secret powers over others, or of others' secret, threatening powers

—can be symptoms of emotional turmoil, too. Returning to such "babyish" behavior as bed-wetting is often a stress signal as well. And persistent stomach troubles (pain, diarrhea, constipation), headaches, fatigue, frequent colds, or other physical symptoms for which a physician can find no bodily cause may be signs of emotional or psychological conflict.

A person whose behavior is wild or erratic, whose mood is constantly bleak and negative, or who can't seem to let go of an irrational idea or fear definitely needs help—and fast. Daniel showed such symptoms before his serious breakdown. If you notice continual worrisome signs in a friend or a relative, whether or not you can take direct action yourself, speak to an adult who can help.

Someone like Alec, whose family thought his troubles were his own fault, may or may not need therapy for himself alone. Focusing on his problems may, in fact, have been his family's way of expressing concern about itself. Still, it was helpful for Alec to be able to voice his gripes openly to someone outside his home instead of creating further trouble for himself by acting out his conflicts.

Unlike Alec, some teens with family difficulties turn inward and become overly concerned about the well-being of their parents or siblings. For them, a few visits with a professional can be a valuable aid in understanding and dealing more realistically with their home situation.

STRESS POINTS

People are especially vulnerable to emotional pain
when they encounter:

- *Change*:
    a move to a new neighborhood, a new
      school, a new life situation
    status shifts: big failures or disappointments,
      big successes
    physical development: rapid growth, big
      weight gains or losses, new appearance
    addition of a family member

- *Loss*:
    death of a family member or friend
    absence of a family member or friend
    divorce in the family

- *Potential change or loss*:
    possible move
    illness of family member or friend
    possible divorce in the family

Anyone who, like Theresa, is going through one
or more stressful life events can benefit from some
kind of therapy just for support. Unfortunately,
many people are not aware of tension in their own
lives or do not think about the physical or behavioral symptoms it can cause. Or they may feel that
expressing or giving in to those symptoms is an act

of weakness—but that is a mistake. Life is full of bumps for everyone. If people seek cushions for those bumps immediately, they are less likely to be bruised or broken in the long run. Therapy at times of crisis is like emergency first aid that prevents a later, possibly worse, infection.

People who have never been in therapy have a hard time believing that if you can get a problem out of your mouth or off your chest in the right way, you can get it out of your life. But for whatever reason, and however it happens, it is true.

In the following chapters are five different examples of how therapy worked for five different teenagers. Although their problems were unique to their lives, how they faced therapy, chose a therapist, and the results they achieved may help answer your own questions about whether you should seek therapy and which kind is right for you.

5

PETER:
INSIGHT THERAPY

Peter knew nothing about psychiatry or psychological theories. He knew a lot about trouble, though.
His family life had been rough and sometimes bru-
tal. He and his older brothers had been in and out
of scrapes for as long as he could remember, and he
had learned how to take punishment so well that it
hardly even scared him. Now he was on the brink of
being in real trouble with the law, and he was afraid
—not of anything the court might do to him, but
because he had been sent to a psychiatrist.

When the door to the psychiatrist's office opened,
Peter expected to see a stern old man with a beard
and a dark suit, or a cold-eyed tough guy like his
school principal. Instead, a youngish man in a tur-
tleneck invited him into a room that was not the
stuffy, mysterious place he had imagined, but a

pleasantly cluttered office decorated with bright pictures. Peter noticed a couch, but the doctor motioned him to a chair and sat in another one, facing Peter.

"I'm Dr. Stone, Peter, and I hear you've been having some trouble."

"Yeah." Peter didn't feel much like talking.

"Well, let's see what we can do to sort things out."

✦ ✦ ✦ ✦

Peter's first introduction to Dr. Stone tells a lot about therapy and therapists that contradicts many people's impressions.

• Psychiatrists don't fit any mold or image. They are men and women like any others, and they come in as wide a variety of shapes and styles as any group of people. Not all therapists look like Sigmund Freud.

• Most young people are used to dealing with adults who have some kind of power over them— parents and authorities like teachers, principals, or, as in Peter's case, law officers. Dr. Stone, though, met Peter face to face. He didn't chew him out or lecture him, but showed that he was interested in him and his problems.

• Although he is a doctor (a physician with special training in psychiatry), Dr. Stone did not set out to "cure" Peter. He was there, as he said, to help him "sort things out." Unlike a medical doctor or a parent, Dr. Stone will not tell Peter what he must do to "get better" or to "act right." When he said, "Let's see what *we* can do . . ." he really meant "we," for therapy is, as you know, a process that involves both the patient and the therapist. It requires working together.

GETTING STARTED

But Peter didn't feel like "working together." There were long silences following Dr. Stone's requests for basic information about Peter's age, grade, and family. Finally the doctor said, "I've heard a lot from everybody and his uncle about what a rotten kid you are. Now I'd like to hear your side of the story—and I want you to know that just about anything you say to me stays with me. The only time I'd have to tell anyone else is if I thought you were going to hurt yourself or some other person. But I don't think that's going to happen."

Unwillingly, Peter began to talk about people always being after him for cutting school, about his pals turning on him when he was in trouble, about his parents always fighting and getting on his back.

"It sounds pretty grim. And you don't much want to be here, do you?"

Peter shook his head.

"I don't blame you, with all those other people

forcing you to come. What would you rather be doing right now?"

"Playing basketball."

Pretty soon, Peter and the doctor were talking basketball—one-on-one, teams, strategies—and before Peter realized it, his hour was up.

"I'd like to see you on Thursday at the same time. Will you be here?"

"Yeah," Peter said.

✦ ✦ ✦ ✦

A psychiatrist or any other therapist will probably talk about "confidentiality" very early on. If not, the patient should ask about it. The general rule is as Dr. Stone told Peter: the confidence is not broken, even to parents, unless the patient seems to be in or to pose real danger. And except for the most extreme cases, a therapist would probably agree to discuss the situation before revealing what someone said in therapy.

Dr. Stone's comment that Peter didn't like being there is the kind of thing that some people might call "mind reading." Obviously, it isn't. Even if he didn't know the facts, even if he were dealing with someone who wasn't *ordered* to his office, Dr. Stone could tell from Peter's choice of words, his tone of voice, his facial expression, and the way he was sitting that the boy was unhappy and uncomfortable. To a therapist, how you say something—or what you *don't* say—is as important as the words you speak. That is one kind of skill that makes therapists better listeners than friends or parents.

Basketball might seem an odd topic of conversation for a session with a psychiatrist. In therapy, however, people find themselves talking about lots of things besides their problems. What they choose to talk about is always important, though. Also, a good therapist *is* interested in what someone enjoys. If Peter were younger, or had trouble dealing with words, Dr. Stone would probably play games with him. Therapists might ask even teenage patients to do something other than talk. Drawing pictures, acting out scenes, or, in some schools of therapy, simple physical exercises are used to release feelings, especially when words come hard. There are limits, though, even in the most "advanced" forms of therapy, to the amount of physical contact between therapist and patient. Patients should speak up if they are asked to do something that makes them uncomfortable.

It was a good sign that at the end of Peter's session he agreed to come back on Thursday. Even though he hadn't wanted to come, after his "hour" (most therapy sessions actually last forty-five or fifty minutes) he found that he didn't mind the thought of returning. This is important, because unless Peter *wants* to participate, he won't get anywhere. One indication of a good therapist is the ability to make someone want to come back after the first one or two sessions, even if those sessions are spent talking only about why he or she didn't want to come!

TESTING, TESTING

After Peter had seen Dr. Stone a few times, the psychiatrist asked that he do something for him— take some tests. Peter panicked. The word *test* is enough to frighten anyone, and Peter especially didn't like the idea of a "psychological test." It made him think that all those rumors about psychiatry were true: that somebody really was going to poke around in his brain.

But Dr. Stone explained that these weren't tests that Peter could "pass" or "fail." They didn't hurt, like some medical tests; in fact, they were sort of fun. They couldn't "poke his brain," but the results (which the doctor would discuss with him) could help show where he and Peter needed to work hardest.

For the tests, Peter went to a psychologist's office. He spent several hours there, drawing pictures, talking about pictures, answering questions out loud and on paper, and trying to solve different kinds of puzzles. When it was over, Peter was tired, but it *hadn't* hurt, and some of it, anyway, had been fun. He had a lot of questions, though, about how some of the almost gamelike tests could possibly reveal anything about him.

◆ ◆ ◆ ◆

By no means does all therapy involve or require testing, but it can be a useful tool in some circumstances. The right kinds of tests—psychological, personality, or intelligence—administered well can help a therapist identify and focus on a patient's most troublesome problems.

If testing is done, it's more likely to precede therapy than to occur during it, as in Peter's case. For example, a student may have taken an intelligence or personality test in school (though fewer and fewer schools are giving such tests), and on the basis of those results, a counselor may recommend therapy. Parents may seek testing for a troubled or troublesome child to find out if therapy is needed or would be useful. Or a clinic may use tests to help determine what form of therapy, if any, would be best for incoming patients.

Not all therapists go over test results with their clients in detail. That would be like telling them what their underlying problems are, and most therapists feel that it's important for patients to discover that knowledge on their own. But a therapist should answer any general questions someone has about a test: "What was this part for?" "What was that part supposed to show?" (But to a question like "What *did* that show about how I feel about my mother?"

a typical therapist's answer would be "What do you think?"!)

It's important to remember that no psychological, intelligence, or personality test is perfect. Some are better designed than others, and there are many different types. Some are given in groups, others individually. Some are done mostly on paper, some require a lot of interaction with the tester. Some are "objective," meaning they present a picture of someone by comparing his or her answers with those of thousands of others who've taken the same test and whose responses have been analyzed. Some are "subjective," meaning the picture consists largely of the impression a person makes on a trained tester. It's important that whoever does the testing, whether a psychologist or some other professional, be well trained. And it is important that no major decision in someone's life be based totally on such tests, because none of them is absolutely accurate.

CLOSE TO THE CORE

As Peter's therapy progressed, it didn't seem to *him* that he was making any progress. It began to bug him that Dr. Stone kept coming back to the same topics, asking questions that Peter had already answered more than once. Some of the doctor's comments—like "Do you know that whenever you talk about your mother you cough?"—really annoyed him.

Who cared? Peter thought. Twice it got to be such a drag that he just didn't show up. And when Dr. Stone wanted to discuss his no-shows, Peter shouted, "Go ahead! Report me! Tell the court! Tell the cops!"

After that session Peter was half afraid that the doctor would report him and half wished that he would. For the next few days he held his breath. But nothing happened, because Dr. Stone did not tell on him. By his next therapy day Peter found, to his surprise, that he was happy to be going.

Peter's feelings and behavior are common reactions to some stages of certain therapies. For example, sometimes there seems to be a lot of repetition. This is part of a process often called "working through": looking at the same topic, conflict, event, idea, or feeling many times from many different angles before finally understanding or resolving it. When this happens, it's no longer a problem.

Like Dr. Stone, most therapists ask questions or make comments that seem silly and can be annoying, usually because they deal with topics people are trying to avoid. Peter's "mother cough," for instance, happened because the thought of his mother bothered him; eventually he was able to admit that, and then to understand why.

Missing appointments as Peter did is called "resistance" in many forms of therapy. This often happens when people get close to subjects they've spent a lot of emotional energy burying or avoiding. Resistance may take the form of missed appointments, lateness, talking at length about irrelevant subjects, insulting the therapist—actions that may not be conscious but that unconsciously serve the purpose of sidestepping the painful nitty-gritty.

Many young people test a therapist in different ways. Like Peter, they may want to find out if the therapist will run to their parents or other authorities. Or they may want to know how much of a pal a therapist really is. Pulling out a joint of marijuana or a can of beer in the office and offering to share it is another way of asking, "Are you really on my side?" Sometimes young people may want their therapist to talk about his or her own teenage experiences. Most good adolescent therapists respond to these tests by making it clear that, though they are on the kids' side, they are adults, and that activities that might (or might not) be appropriate among friends are not properly shared with them.

Peter's angry outburst at Dr. Stone is what many forms of therapy, particularly insight therapies, refer to as "acting out." These schools believe patients express their feelings about important people and conflicts in their lives using the therapist as a target in a process called "transference." In Peter's case, the buried feeling was rage, especially about the way his father had treated him. Dr. Stone would say that Peter "transferred" his feelings about his father to him, and that his patient felt much safer yelling at his therapist than at the cause of his painful emotions.

Peter's insight therapy is not psychoanalysis, although Dr. Stone used many analytic techniques. True psychoanalysis focuses less on problem-solving than on the dissection of the character and the psyche by specialists trained in Freud's very specific theories and methods. Analysis tends to be long and intensive (and usually expensive), and although it is not a common form of therapy for teens, there are analysts who specialize in helping adolescents probe into their personalities.

Peter's treatment will go on for a while because his problems started early, have grown deep roots, and are causing him a lot of trouble. We'll catch up with him later, but in the meantime let's examine a different form of therapy as Janet experienced it.

6
JANET: BEHAVIORIST THERAPY

Fifteen-year-old Janet's feelings of general misery and wretchedness finally overcame her timidity about seeking therapy. She found a therapist by calling the local mental-health society, which referred her to a private social-service agency.

She felt nervous even making that first phone call for information, and even more timid about calling the agency for an appointment. Maybe she was just being silly, she told herself, and she put off calling. But one morning she woke up feeling so sad and rotten that she marched to the phone and did it. Now she was glad she had. She was about to have her second meeting with Mrs. Kamm, a social worker, and she was looking forward to it.

✦ ✦ ✦ ✦

Janet's shyness about contacting a therapist is, as you know from Chapter 1, a common occurrence. The way she finally made her move is common, too; people often live with a problem, major or minor, for a long time (or for what seems to be a long time) until they feel they can't cope by themselves and must reach out for help. This happens at different times and in different ways for different people and situations, but it is a turning point that many people in therapy can describe.

Although Peter in the last chapter had a male therapist and Janet was assigned to a female therapist, gender matching isn't a requirement in therapy. According to some therapists and therapeutic theories, teenagers should have therapists of their own sex, largely because of the modeling process that goes on while adolescents are learning adult roles. Most professionals, though, are not rigid about this. Janet was assigned to Mrs. Kamm by the agency's "intake officer"—the person who interviews prospective patients to get a general view of their problems and personalities—because she seemed to be the staff member who was best suited to Janet's needs. Janet would soon agree. Right away she felt comfortable with the tall and attractive Mrs. Kamm, for reasons that would later become clear. Because the way someone relates to his or her therapist can be crucial, Janet's feelings about Mrs. Kamm were a positive sign of things to come.

ZEROING IN

During their first meeting, Janet felt so good about Mrs. Kamm that she had no trouble stating her problem: "I'm just miserable, that's all."

"You do look pretty unhappy," replied the therapist, "but can you give me some more details? What are you miserable about?"

"For one thing, I don't have any friends."

"None?"

"Hardly any—only Laura, now, and she's been ignoring me. Besides, nobody wants to hang around with a loser—and I mess up everything I try!"

They spent the rest of the session further exploring Janet's misery. Toward the end, Mrs. Kamm asked Janet if her parents knew that she had come for help.

"No—they'd only laugh at me," Janet answered.

"Well, I'd like you to come back next week at the same time. In the meantime, I want you to tell your parents what you are doing. Also, from now on I want you to be aware of every incident that proves you have no friends, and every failure that makes you unhappy. Write them down if you want to. We'll talk about them next week. If you want to phone me during the week, please do. We even have a recording machine that takes messages during the night. Okay?"

"Okay."

✦ ✦ ✦ ✦

Like Janet, many people who seek therapy know only that they are unhappy; they don't know why. This is often especially true of young people, who haven't had as much experience with life's troubles. In these cases, a therapist needs to help narrow the problem to some specific issues that can be focused on. That was Mrs. Kamm's goal with Janet's "homework" assignment.

As you may have noticed, Mrs. Kamm's way of dealing with Janet is different from Dr. Stone's with Peter. This is partly because they were trained differently: Mrs. Kamm learned to take more of a behaviorist approach; Dr. Stone relies mainly on "insight." In addition, Mrs. Kamm is a different person with her own style, and Janet's situation is quite unlike Peter's. Janet's problems are not as long-standing, and she needs support and guidance more than analysis. The differences between Mrs. Kamm and Dr. Stone and between Peter and Janet point up the importance of making sure the therapist selected suits a particular person's needs.

As early as the first meeting, it is a good idea to find out if a therapist is available for calls between sessions and how he or she can be reached. Any kind of psychological treatment may stir up unexpected emotion that just can't wait until "next week." If Janet needed someone to talk to, for instance, Mrs. Kamm made it clear how to get in touch with her.

What about the parental issue? Whether parents must be informed of, or must give permission for, therapy depends on someone's age, situation, and residence. (See page 127 for sources of information about legal rights, and pages 129-130 for sources of informal counseling.) Depending upon a locality's laws, it is possible, for example, for a teenager to go to a free or low-cost clinic or counseling center without his or her parents ever knowing about it. Mrs. Kamm was not required to ask Janet to tell her parents; she simply thought it would be best for Janet's sake.

TAKING ACTION

At their next session, Janet was happy to see Mrs. Kamm again. She had been working hard and had a list that proved she was right to be "miserable."

Mrs. Kamm noticed that Janet looked happy, but that the hem of her skirt was torn, there was a spot on her shirt, her hair needed washing, and her shoulders slumped. "Did you tell your parents about me?" she asked.

Janet had, and her parents hadn't laughed—in fact, they had seemed almost proud. And why, she was asked, had she thought they would laugh?

"They just always act like I can't take care of my-self or make up my own mind about anything" was the response. At Mrs. Kamm's request, Janet ex-plained that her parents wanted to know where she was going, where she'd been, and what she was planning to do next—and they always seemed to propose a "better suggestion."

Then the therapist asked for Janet's report on her week. As Janet recited her list, Mrs. Kamm asked a few questions. None of Janet's classmates had in-vited her to do anything after school or over the weekend—but no, she hadn't invited anyone either. She'd made a report in class and nobody had lis-tened—but no, she hadn't spent much time on it. She'd volunteered to organize a class bake sale and it had been a total washout—but no, she didn't much like cooking.

"Those things must have made you feel miserable indeed," Mrs. Kamm commented. "Why do you think you're so thoroughly ignored?"

Janet had a hard time getting the answer out of her mouth. In fact, she was almost crying when she said, "I guess they just don't like the way I look!"

With Mrs. Kamm's help, Janet was able to explain that she was "too tall" and felt like "an oaf." At five feet six inches, she was already four inches taller than her mother.

"I know how you feel, Janet," Mrs. Kamm sympa-thized. "When I was your age, I *hated* being tall, and I slumped, just the way you do—I thought it would make me look shorter. Is that why you don't stand up straight?"

"I guess so." It made Janet feel good that somebody—especially somebody as nice as Mrs. Kamm—had been through the same trouble.

"Now, I have another assignment. This week I want you to invite at least one friend over to your house. I want you to do your homework extra carefully in at least one subject. And if the opportunity comes up, I want you to volunteer to do something you'll really enjoy. Then tell me what happens."

Janet was on her way out of the office when Mrs. Kamm added, "Oh—and try this, too: every day, make sure that your clothes look neat and your hair is clean."

"Why?" Janet was beginning to get irritated.

"We'll talk about it next week."

✦ ✦ ✦ ✦

Although she was not aware of it, a lot of Janet's worries had to do with the "normal craziness" of being a teenager. Simply the fact of rapid growth, for example, can cause confusion. Janet felt uncomfortable with her body in part because it was so "new"; for her, as for many teens, bad feelings about her physical self extended to a negative view of her entire self. Although her body was fast becoming that of an adult, her parents still treated her like a child, and that only added to Janet's misery. In her case, just hearing from an unrelated adult that she wasn't as weird as she felt was a big help. Then why did she leave Mrs. Kamm's office feeling annoyed?

GAINING STRENGTH

At her third session, Janet looked better. Not only was she a lot tidier, but she was standing straighter and her face looked more relaxed than usual. She reported to Mrs. Kamm that she had invited Laura over and they'd had a fun Saturday afternoon together. She'd really read her history assignments and had been praised for her classwork. She had volunteered to watch a neighbor's children and ended up with a regular baby-sitting job—and her mother had congratulated her for this.

"Fine, Janet! You must be pleased! And why do you think you had all that success?"

At first Janet didn't have an answer to Mrs. Kamm's questions, but by the end of the session she had begun to realize that the difference between the past week and the one before that was that *she* had made a sensible effort to succeed. Her assignment for the following week was the same as before, and in addition, Mrs. Kamm asked her to think about this question: if you succeed when you try to succeed, what is it that makes you fail?

✦ ✦ ✦ ✦

In addition to giving support and understanding, Mrs. Kamm was practicing a form of behavior modification. By asking Janet first to examine her life in terms of specific misery-causing actions or behavior, and then to change some of these actions, piece by piece, she was helping Janet find new ways of behaving that should, at the same time, make a difference in her feelings.

Janet was willing to cooperate with Mrs. Kamm because, without realizing it, she had "identified" with her therapist, a too-tall teen who was now an attractive, confident woman. Such identification often occurs during therapy, and some schools of thought place great emphasis on the importance of this kind of close relationship between patient and therapist.

DIGGING DEEPER

"But it doesn't make *sense* to try to fail on purpose!" Janet announced at the beginning of the next meeting. She had been thinking hard about Mrs. Kamm's question.

That day and for several more sessions, patient and therapist talked about why someone like Janet might set herself up for failure. Finally Janet came to the following conclusions:

• Adolescence is a scary time for some people, and "failing"—especially when it can be made to seem like someone else's fault—can be a way to escape the responsibilities of growing up.

• She felt ugly and presented a poor appearance so that others might easily agree. She set things up, however, so that she could pretend she was mistreated for reasons other than being unattractive.

• She felt she was a disappointment in her parents' eyes, and she imagined that they were rejecting her because of this. Instead of expressing her anger toward them, she did her best, unconsciously, to get back at them by failing.

After this session, there were a few more meetings and a few more assignments. Then Mrs. Kamm declared that Janet was ready to stop therapy because she had solved her problems and had learned what had caused them. Although this made Janet proud, it made her nervous, too, so she was relieved to hear that she could call on Mrs. Kamm again for help if she needed it.

◆ ◆ ◆ ◆

Janet's understanding of herself may not seem sensible to you—and it may not be helpful for anyone else, even for anyone with symptoms like Janet's. Each of us has our own inner logic; each of us operates on the basis of unique conscious and unconscious motives. What matters is that Janet's new understanding of herself made sense to *her*. This is true for anyone in therapy.

Like most adolescent therapy, Janet's was brief

and involved little time digging through dreams and events of her past. This is because, as one psychiatrist puts it, "The problems one usually sees in teenagers are blockages to growth. It is usually the therapist's job to help the young person remove those blockages, and then simply let growth go on." Often, too, teens are changing too fast to have much patience or need for long-term treatment.

Janet's therapy moved quickly, also, because she wanted to do it, and because she worked hard at it during the sessions and in between. In addition, she sought help before her problems were buried too deeply or too wrapped up in other parts of her life. These are important points for someone considering or entering therapy to remember.

Ending therapy is tricky. Someone pushed as hard into therapy as Peter was may not have a choice about when to stop. Parents who are not as supportive of therapy as Janet's were may pressure their child to end sessions too soon, especially if they are expensive. There also may be times when a patient strongly feels that he or she is ready to quit, but the therapist disagrees. This *may* mean that instead of understanding troublesome issues, the patient is trying to avoid them—that "resistance" we talked about in the last chapter.

Janet's termination, however, was very satisfactory: her therapist told her that she was ready to stop, and even though she was nervous, Janet had to agree. Agreeing is important. If she had any doubts about Mrs. Kamm's recommendation to end her sessions, she should have voiced them. And if her therapist had not volunteered the information, she should have asked if it was okay to contact her after therapy was "over."

In fact, Janet did talk with Mrs. Kamm several times during the following year when she hit some rough spots. It made her feel good to know that she had someone outside her family and friends to whom she could turn. It made her feel even better to know that she had gained a new outlook on herself, her life, and her behavior that would always be useful. She knew, too, that if she ever felt the need for help again, she wouldn't be timid about asking for it.

7
ALEC: FAMILY THERAPY

Unlike Janet, the last thing in the world that thirteen-year-old Alec wanted was therapy. In fact, Alec was furious. Sure, he'd been having some problems at school—but so was almost everyone else he knew in junior high school. Of course, he'd been giving his parents a hard time lately. Who wouldn't? Especially if they and other family members are bent on ruining your life! So what happens? His parents punish him by hauling him to a "shrink"! As if he didn't have enough cranky adults to deal with already. As if he were crazy!

Dr. Barclay, a psychologist whose practice included family therapy, listened to Alec's story. His parents were always bickering, he said, but whenever *he* did or said anything the least bit critical, they

84

lectured him for not showing "respect." It burned him up so much that he felt like exploding!

"Is that what's been happening in school—you explode?" Dr. Barclay asked. She had already read the teachers' reports and test results Alec's parents had brought.

"Yeah, I guess. Then, whenever I get into trouble, they say, 'Why can't you be good, like your sister?' My sister! The little creep . . ."

Dr. Barclay made no comment but told Alec, "I'm going to be meeting with your parents tomorrow. Don't worry, I won't pass along anything you've said today; but I do want to find out how they view all this. Then we'll see what we can do to work things out. Thanks for coming, Alec."

Dr. Barclay is a psychologist in private practice, meaning that she has a kind of "therapy business," counseling individual clients or families for a fee in an office of her own. Psychologists may also work in clinics, hospitals, or schools, and some concentrate more on giving psychological tests than on therapy.

She could not have read Alec's school reports without his parents' help. Laws vary from state to state and change over time, but the general rule is that school records—test results, teachers' reports, and the like—remain confidential unless the student or the student's parents ask to see them or give permission to have them released to someone else.

In Alec's case, the school records proved to be quite important because they gave Dr. Barclay a view of Alec that was fairly objective and, she would discover, that differed from his parents' description and his own complaints. The records showed her a picture of a young man who was basically stable, fairly bright, generally well liked, and usually a good student. During the last year, though, he'd been having trouble: his grades dropped sharply, and his teachers had grown critical of his behavior. These indicated to Dr. Barclay that something in Alec's life had recently upset him.

By asking Alec about his "explosions," she planted the seeds for helping him see the connection between his behavior and his feelings. Like many people, Alec didn't yet realize that "invisible" emotions can influence or control "visible" behavior or physical sensations.

Did you notice that the psychologist made no comment when Alec talked about his sister? Dr. Stone might have poked and probed at that kind of statement from Peter. Mrs. Kamm might have said something like "That must be very hard for you" if Janet had expressed a similar feeling. But Dr. Barclay wasn't sure yet that Alec was her patient;

she didn't want to rally to his side or anyone else's side until she had gotten to know Alec's whole family.

MORE THAN ONE PATIENT

"What's wrong with him, Doctor?" Alec's father, Jim Foster, asked at the beginning of the parents' conference with Dr. Barclay.

"It's really too early to say," she replied. "I gather, though, that there has been some kind of upheaval at home. Could you tell me something about that?"

Mr. Foster described his recent job troubles and his disagreements with his wife over her working even part-time to help out. These tensions often erupted into arguments. "Then Alec picks this of all times to start acting up!" he complained. "Just when I feel I need some respect and consideration, he refuses to give it!"

"Our daughter, Pat, who is only eleven, has been very cooperative and understanding," Mrs. Foster added. "That's what makes us so concerned about Alec."

"He's at an age when life can be very confusing," the doctor explained, "and that combined with the tensions at home may make things even harder for him. I doubt that there is anything seriously the matter with Alec, but you're all having a difficult time. So I'd suggest that we all work together in family sessions."

✦ ✦ ✦ ✦

The Fosters were not hostile to the idea of therapy, and they agreed to be treated as a family. Despite their money worries, expense was not a problem because Mr. Foster's medical insurance covered much of the fee.

The Fosters' interest in therapy was possible, in part, because they could afford it. Before beginning any kind of treatment, it's important to find out what expenses, if any, will be covered by an insurance or other medical plan. This is especially true for young people interested in treatment whose parents or guardians balk at the cost. If the Fosters' therapy had not been covered, they could have gone to a free or low-cost clinic, mental-health center, or social-service agency, where family therapy is also available.

Alec's parents' version of their family situation was obviously quite different from Alec's. That's why Dr. Barclay wanted at least to confer with them. Most therapists who work with young people spend some time with their parents. A few limit these contacts to conversations held only at the parents' request; some will formally treat one or both parents on an individual basis or recommend that parents seek their own therapy. Still others will arrange conferences with parents at various points during their child's therapy in order to give support, advice, or guidance. These conferences do not include "reports" on any conversations or other specifics unless the child has given the therapist permission.

Not all therapists practice family therapy. Some object to the very idea of it, because it goes against their professional training or does not fit the theories of their psychological schools. Others may approve of treating the family as a unit but may not have the training or experience for the special skills required.

Dr. Barclay had both, and she suggested family therapy because she felt Alec was what some therapists call the "designated patient." It seemed to Dr. Barclay that the whole Foster family was troubled but that it was Alec who was being blamed as the cause. Therapists have found that designated patients are often young (or very old) family members; frequently they are teenagers who may be going through and dishing out what turn out to be just typical adolescent difficulties.

GETTING STARTED

One of the first decisions to be made had to do with names. Dr. Barclay asked that they work with each other on a first-name basis: all the Fosters would call her Helen, and she would address them as Jim, Fran, Pat, and Alec.

The next decision was where they would meet. They finally agreed that some time would be spent in the Fosters' home and some in Dr. Barclay's office. Though the therapist would usually want to see all of them together, if it seemed useful, she would speak to them in twos or threes or individually.

✦ ✦ ✦ ✦

Although Helen Barclay thinks that first names help her seem like part of the family, other therapists want to keep the distance that the use of last names and titles encourages. Attitudes about names vary from therapist to therapist regardless of their school, but therapists generally call young people by their first names. If someone is unsure of how to address a therapist, the only thing to do is ask.

Not all family therapists visit the home. Those who do feel that it helps them get a clearer idea of how a particular family operates in its own setting. Although people can feel uneasy at first, a good therapist knows how to make family members relax and behave normally despite the presence of a stranger.

Not all family therapists have sessions with individuals, either. Some hold only group meetings, whereas others, like Helen Barclay, set up a regular routine of group sessions combined with individual ones.

FIRSTHAND OBSERVATIONS

At the beginning of her work with the Fosters, Dr. Barclay stayed somewhat in the background, observing the family without comment. Soon, though, she became much more involved. Not only did she ask many questions, but when the Fosters were talking or arguing among themselves, she would intervene: "Alec's remark seemed to make you angry, Jim. Why?" "Fran, how did you feel when Jim used that tone of voice to you?" "Pat, why aren't you talking?"

During countless exchanges over the next few months, Dr. Barclay could see a clear pattern of unproductive behavior. Gradually she was able to help the Fosters see the pattern, too. One technique she used was role-playing: having one family member act the part of another. During each scene Dr. Barclay encouraged the actors to say out loud how someone else's words or actions made them *feel*. Although performing made the Fosters uncomfortable at first, their uneasiness was soon replaced by fascination, as they discovered emotions and behavioral habits that they didn't know existed.

Once when Alec and Pat played the roles of their parents, for instance, the older Fosters heard "themselves" arguing about money. As his father, Alec complained that Fran was obviously spending too much on groceries, since she'd served steak for dinner. Speaking for her mother, Pat said, "First you make a fuss about my looking for a job; then you won't let me do the job I have now, taking care of the family! It makes me feel so helpless!"

Dr. Barclay also used role-playing to help the Fosters learn healthier ways of dealing with one another. She did this by asking the "actors" after each scene to describe how they would have preferred the situation to be handled.

✦ ✦ ✦ ✦

Of course, every family's therapy is different because every family is different. Role-playing is only one of many techniques that may be used. (Role-playing also occurs in other kinds of therapy.) Usually, though, a family therapist is more active and openly involved than other helping professionals. This is because family members often deal with one another in ways of which they may be unaware. A therapist may need to point out these behaviors and the impact they have on other family members in order to make a change in the home situation.

UNDERSTANDING FAMILY PRESSURES

After about a year of twice-weekly sessions, the Fosters were able to understand their family conflicts. Mr. Foster recognized that the pressure he felt from his work troubles was worsened because he'd been brought up to believe that supporting the family was a "man's job." During this rough time Alec reached adolescence, when a certain of amount of rebellion is normal—but Mr. Foster interpreted Alec's behavior as disrespect and as yet another threat to his status.

Mrs. Foster learned that enduring her husband's irritability was doubly hard for her because she felt so helpless: not only could she not get a moneymaking job without stirring up trouble, but because the kids were older, she had fewer responsibilities in her job at home. As a result, she began to resent her husband; Dr. Barclay helped her see that instead of taking her resentment out on him directly, she got into emotional fights over "nothing" and became especially critical of Alec.

Alec was relieved to find out through the sessions with Dr. Barclay that some of his trouble was "normal," but he also came to understand that sometimes he acted badly because his father's situation made *him* nervous. Therapy also helped him realize that his sister was "good" by comparison partly because of her younger age and partly because she was naturally quieter and more polite. Finally, he concluded that, whether it was a question of "respect" or not, he really owed his worried father a bit more consideration.

In fact, the whole Foster family learned to compromise. Mrs. Foster got a part-time job, and everyone began pitching in around the house. For the Fosters, change and adjustment came fairly easily; sometimes the process is much more painful and difficult. The fact that they were all receptive to therapy helped ensure its effectiveness and smoothness.

In addition to situations like the Fosters', when the whole family has trouble getting along, family therapy can be useful when a single member has a serious problem, such as a mental, emotional, or physical disorder that the rest of the household must learn to live with and around. Sometimes, though, a home situation is just the reverse—one family member must learn to live with and around turmoil. For people caught in troubles like these, the support offered by other therapies can be valuable, as the next chapter, about Theresa, will show.

8
THERESA: CRISIS-INTERVENTION THERAPY

Theresa was confused. Her family had recently moved to a new neighborhood, her grandmother had just died, and her parents had separated. She was having trouble sleeping, and headaches were interfering with her concentration at school, but it hadn't occurred to her that these problems were connected. Then a teacher sent her to the school guidance counselor, who suggested that she "spend some time with a specialist who could provide extra support during this troublesome period."

What did that mean? Theresa wondered. A psychiatrist? Years and years on a couch? She wasn't insane, she thought, she just needed sleep! She was sure a specialist couldn't help, and besides, she felt her mother had enough troubles already without a therapist's bill. Anyway, she was old enough, she thought, to be learning how to live with and through her difficulties.

So Theresa didn't follow up on the guidance counselor's suggestion. During the next few weeks, though, her schoolwork fell further in quality, which Theresa still blamed on her lack of sleep.

Luckily the counselor was persistent. He called her in again and set up a meeting for her and her mother with Mr. Griffin, the psychologist who periodically visited Theresa's school. At that conference Mr. Griffin spent some time talking with Theresa and going through her school records. Then he spoke with her mother and referred them both to the town's community mental-health center. He recommended, though, that Theresa first be examined by a physician to make sure that the insomnia and headaches had no physical cause.

✦ ✦ ✦ ✦

Theresa's apprehensions about therapy and her grin-and-bear-it attitude toward personal problems are, as you know, quite common. But it is at times of crisis—at major turning points in our lives—that therapy can be the most valuable. Everyone needs support at these times, and the right kind of support can keep a temporary difficulty from getting buried and returning later as a serious problem. Theresa also didn't know that "therapy" during a short-lived crisis is least likely to involve couches or the other elements of psychiatry that seem to frighten people the most. Instead, it can be as simple as sharing one's feelings on a regular basis with a person or a group familiar with the troublesome situation.

Theresa was fortunate. Few schools have full-time staff psychologists; many don't even have access to the services of a visiting psychologist and instead rely completely on a guidance counselor (who may or may not have psychological training) to detect and deal with students' emotional problems.

No school psychologist or guidance counselor, though, has the time to give in-depth therapy. As a result, their views of a student's state of mind or emotional condition should not be taken as the final word, especially if an important decision (such as a change of schools or hospital treatment) needs to be made. Still, they are very useful as sources of information on where, how, and when to seek further aid. They can refer people to reliable providers of therapy or support, and they can advise parents, which, as in Theresa's case, can be an important role. Even parents who may not at first like the idea of psychotherapy may be willing to consider it if a professional connected with their child's school suggests it. And someone like Mr. Griffin (not Dr. Griffin; he has a master's degree rather than a doctorate in psychology), who spends most of his working time with young people, has the advantage of being quite familiar with what problems fall within the "normal" range for teenagers and what are serious enough to merit special help.

His advice that Theresa see a physician was absolutely correct—and it can't be repeated too often. For although many physical symptoms can be the result of emotional stress, they may also have physical causes and so deserve a thorough checkup. In addition, problems that appear to be "mental" or emotional often are in fact caused by physical abnormalities, ranging from minor brain damage to hormone imbalances. Finally, worry over physical symptoms may only increase stress and emotional turmoil. These days, more mental-health professionals are alert to physical causes of disorders, and more physicians are aware of emotional causes of physical symptoms. Even so, someone with unexplainable physical or emotional symptoms would be wise to consult a "body doctor" along with a "head doctor."

CLINIC COUNSELING

At the community mental-health center, Theresa and her mother were interviewed about Theresa's background and symptoms. Theresa's mother was reassured to learn that her daughter's reactions to the recent "bumps" in her life were common and nothing to feel frightened or guilty about. She was also glad to find out that the cost of Theresa's treatment would be low, and that if she would fill out some financial forms it might be free.

After that intake interview, Theresa saw Rachel Lewis, a rather young psychologist who had some training but who was working toward an advanced degree. They met twice a week for three weeks.

"It must be very hard coping with so many big, complicated changes at once," Rachel said at their first session. Finally, Theresa was able to admit, out loud, that it *was* hard.

During the course of Theresa's therapy, Rachel would say things like "Many people your age would be very angry at their parents for divorcing." "I imagine it was pretty frightening when your grandmother died." "I remember when my family moved to a new town; I was sure I'd never have another friend—it was so depressing!" These kinds of comments always made it easier for Theresa to talk about how she felt about the divorce, the death, and the move in her own life.

✦ ✦ ✦ ✦

Like Rachel Lewis, many therapists and counselors are "still in school." They must have reached a certain level in their education and training to be allowed to practice, even within an organization like a mental-health clinic, but the fact that they are still learning needn't be a drawback. In fact, it can be a positive sign that they are interested enough in their profession to pursue it further. Also, if someone is still in training, he or she probably works with a supervisor. That can be an advantage, too, because a trainee's caseload gets the attention of two therapists, one especially enthusiastic and one extra-experienced. Of course, cases are discussed in supervisory sessions, but the information goes no further than the supervisor.

Theresa's form of therapy is called crisis intervention, which means it deals with one or more very specific problems in a person's life. These might include a death or a birth in the family, a divorce, a remarriage, a move, or an illness. The purpose of crisis intervention is to provide support, information, and a sounding board in the form of someone or a group not directly involved in the troublesome situation.

You may notice that Rachel was very direct in her comments. She didn't probe subtly for Theresa's feelings, but made statements and asked precise questions to give Theresa the chance to express emotions that someone else clearly understood. Often, all that is needed during a crisis is for someone to say, "It's okay to feel whatever you're feeling." Sometimes this makes it easier to talk about worries and in this way clears up any emotional or physical effects they might be causing. This worked for Theresa, at any rate: after one or two sessions with Rachel Lewis, she soon began sleeping better and her headaches went away without pills.

GROUP SESSIONS

After a few more talks, Rachel suggested that Theresa sit in on a "divorced-kids group" that met one afternoon a week at the community center. The group was made up of kids, all about Theresa's age, whose parents were just going through a separation or divorce, or who had been "divorced kids" for a good while. George, a social worker, sat with the group and did some talking, mostly in the form of questions. Mainly, however, the kids talked.

At first Theresa felt a bit shy. But after she had listened for a while, she began to feel as if she'd known these people for a long time, because so many of their feelings and experiences sounded familiar. Also, it was good to hear the more "seasoned" members of the group talk; they made her realize that life after a divorce would indeed settle down sometime!

Soon she began to contribute to the conversation. "My folks just split up a few months ago. I thought it was going to be terrible, but I found out it wasn't. In fact, I almost like it better because there's no fighting. Did anybody else notice that?"

✦ ✦ ✦ ✦

There are many different kinds of therapeutic groups. Some, like Theresa's, consist of people who share a common problem. They are able to learn from each other (and from whatever leader there is) and to give each other support. Some community centers or Y's have ongoing "teen groups" where kids can drop in and just talk over their problems. There they can get advice and sometimes useful criticism from people their own age. Some of these groups have leaders; others are just rap sessions. Check around your community for something like it if you feel you could use somebody to talk to.

More formal groups are organized by therapists who conduct them according to the ideas of their particular psychological training. Participants in these sessions may also be in individual therapy or may go only to "group."

Under good leadership, group therapy can help people learn more about themselves as well as how to relate better to others, not only through special therapeutic techniques but through feedback from group members, too. The only drawbacks to group therapy are those that apply to any form of therapy: in the wrong hands it can do more harm than good. So it's advisable to take part only in groups run by a recognized therapist or by an organization with a reliable reputation.

✦ ✦ ✦ ✦

Theresa gained from her group the ability to talk about her problems and her emotions with "ordinary people." She got support, but she also learned not to feel sorry for herself. Although Rachel had been helpful, and Theresa knew that she could always turn to her for a sympathetic ear, it was important for Theresa to be able to deal openly with her crises and concerns. Discovering that other people shared similar worries helped a lot. Besides, she made a bunch of new friends!

9
DANIEL: CRISIS INTERVENTION AND RESIDENTIAL TREATMENT

Daniel had been acting so strangely that his girl friend Sally was really worried. He said things that didn't make any sense, and he did peculiar things, too—like laughing wildly when nothing funny was going on. At first she thought that he was on drugs, and when he denied it, she was hurt because she was sure he was lying to her. When one day he calmly explained that it wasn't drugs that made him act that way, but the "echo voices" that were all around him, she grew frightened and decided to end the relationship.

She planned to tell him so that night, after their date at a drive-in movie. But when the show was over, he just sat, and Sally realized that he'd been sitting that way, without moving, for nearly an hour. She couldn't make him move, either, so she squeezed in next to him, started the car herself, and

104

headed for the hospital emergency room. A police officer stopped her because she was driving strangely, but when he understood what was going on, he helped her get Daniel to the hospital.

✦ ✦ ✦ ✦

Symptoms like Daniel's are what often come to mind when people think of "craziness." *Crazy* is a scary word, but Daniel was indeed sick. His kind of illness can sometimes be related to the use of drugs, or it can have other causes within the mind or body of the sufferer. Whatever the cause, Sally was right to head for the emergency room because Daniel's symptoms called for immediate action and his illness would require intensive, constant care.

The first treatment offered in cases like Daniel's is called crisis intervention, the same label applied to the type of therapy that Theresa, in the last chapter, received. Daniel's treatment, however, was different in form, just as his crisis was obviously different from Theresa's. In Daniel's situation, "intervention" refers to the quick action taken by the hospital emergency-room staff once they realized that Daniel was in serious trouble.

EMERGENCY PROCEDURES

While a staff psychiatrist cared for Daniel, other hospital personnel tried to reach his parents by phone. When they finally arrived at the hospital, they were angry; they assumed that the police were harassing their "little boy" or that there was some mistake. But after the doctors and Sally described what had happened, their anger changed to fear and distress, and they had to be calmed down in order to give permission for Daniel's admission to the hospital.

Once Daniel had been settled into a room in the psychiatric ward, his parents had another conference with the psychiatrist. At first they maintained that they were totally surprised by this terrifying breakdown, but gradually they began to recall and piece together Daniel's rather odd behavior of the last six months.

✦ ✦ ✦ ✦

Although state laws vary (check with the organizations on page 127), the general rule is that no minor (a person under a certain age, usually eighteen) can be given medical treatment or admitted to a hospital without the permission of a parent or guardian. Considering Daniel's condition (and the fact that the police were involved), the hospital was within its rights in holding him until Daniel's parents were located. Under some circumstances—and again, state laws vary—he could have been committed to the psychiatric ward against his will on the authority of a certain number of doctors, the police, or a judge and kept there for a short time, even if his parents had not given permission.

Daniel's parents were probably not lying when they expressed surprise at their son's condition. Often people who are closest to a problem, even a severe one, don't notice it. They get used to the strange behavior, perhaps, or assume that it's just a "normal part of growing up." Or they may be so frightened that they pretend there's nothing wrong, fearing the cause even more.

It took a lot of courage for Sally to do what she did. If you see a friend or relative acting strangely, especially in ways that are not so dramatic as Daniel's, it can be hard to bring the subject up. But it's the nicest favor you can ever do for a friend to ask, "Have you ever thought of asking the counselor for some advice?" Or say, "Here's the phone number for a hotline—I called them once when I felt really rotten, and they helped a lot." Most communities have many resources for psychological emergencies. Hospitals, hotlines, mental-health centers, suicide-prevention bureaus, the police and fire departments—all are there to help and be used! (See pages 129-130 for more details.)

IN THE HOSPITAL

Daniel's problem was diagnosed as a psychosis, or a severe mental abnormality that separates the sufferer from reality. Many psychoses can be treated with a combination of drugs and psychotherapy, but (especially during the "acute" phases of such disorders when the symptoms become most severe) the patient must be prevented from injuring himself or others, so hospitalization is often called for.

After a couple of nights in the local psychiatric ward, Daniel was moved to a hospital that specializes in mental diseases. By that time, partly because of the medication he had received, he was aware of what was going on, and he really resisted the idea of "being put away." His parents insisted, though, because they were now convinced of the seriousness of his illness, and they knew they couldn't help him at home.

Although he didn't like it at first, the hospital wasn't as bad as Daniel had imagined it would be. He lived in a wing reserved for people his age, where he followed a daily schedule that included a combination of all the different kinds of therapy described so far, plus a few others. He had individual sessions with a therapist and regular, formal group sessions led by a psychologist. All the kids in the wing met in both small and large groups for what were really rap sessions about daily problems. A physician and other medical personnel kept tabs on his physical condition, and his body chemistry was regularly monitored to check the effects of his medication. In addition, there were other activities, including sports, crafts, music—and, yes, school.

◆ ◆ ◆ ◆

"Mental hospital" stirs up frightening images in most people of any age. All are not like the one that Daniel went to (some, for instance, mix young and old people by grouping them according to their disorder rather than their age), but most today are not the unpleasant places many of us imagine. Still, nobody likes to be kept in a place against his or her will; and in most states parents may commit a child who is a minor to a mental institution even if the child objects (though in most states a young person may appeal a court-ordered commitment).

The psychiatric institution where Daniel was committed, however, seemed to be ideal for someone Daniel's age and for his particular problems. Not only was it a reasonably pleasant place to live, but it also offered activities and therapies specifically geared to young people. There was a good proportion of staff members, from psychiatrists through recreation leaders, who were experienced in dealing with teenagers. The staff was willing to show Daniel's parents and other visitors through the facilities, answer their questions, and explain treatment processes as well. Although Daniel's mother and father would surely check on any of their son's complaints, on the surface, anyway, it appeared he was receiving excellent care.

READJUSTING

After a few months, Daniel was ready to leave the hospital. The symptoms of his disease were well under control, and through his therapy he'd come to understand what had happened to him. It took some time for him to be able to admit that he had been terrified for months before his psychotic break, when his separation from reality became dramatically apparent. Once he got to that point in his therapy, though, it wasn't hard for him to confront the facts and sort them out.

Leaving the hospital, however, didn't mean he was ready to return to his old routine. Instead, he went for a time to a halfway house—a residence or dormitory where he, along with a small group of other previously disturbed teens, prepared for reentry into "normal" life. This residential treatment involved learning how to cope with the new demands their hospitalization had placed on their lives and relearning old and important habits.

In the meantime, Daniel's parents were receiving therapy, too. They had to deal with the guilt and fear they felt about their son's illness, and they would need additional support and guidance when he came back home. For Daniel's life and their own would not be exactly the same as before, at least not right away. He would have to continue his medication and therapy, and his family would need to give him extra care and help as well.

✦ ✦ ✦ ✦

Residential treatment of psychiatric problems, in combination with brief hospitalization or by itself, is frequently useful for young people. Sometimes therapists may recommend that even teens without severe illnesses live away from home for a time. Their home situation may be causing their problems, for example; or their symptoms may be so upsetting to their families that it is better for them to receive therapy away from home.

Retraining at a halfway house, like Daniel's, is essential for anyone who has gone through an experience as distressing as his or who has been out of touch with the outside world for a while. Any illness like Daniel's can be terrifying and unsettling. A halfway house gives people a chance to feel sure of themselves again and of their ability to survive in the everyday world.

All of this help is, as you might imagine, quite expensive. Health insurance may pay for all or most of it, though, as Daniel's family policy did. Also, this kind of absolutely vital treatment is often available at little or no cost from public or nonprofit sources. For instance, Daniel might have gotten treatment on an outpatient basis from a city hospital after a brief stay in the hospital.

The therapy for Daniel's parents was also vital, both for their sake and for his. Living with a person with psychiatric or emotional problems, or with a person who is going through therapy for any reason, can be difficult. We'll talk more about this in the next chapter.

10
THERAPY'S SIDE EFFECTS

If you are in therapy, it can be hard to remember that you are not the only person experiencing change. You may not be fully aware of how much you are changing, but it is happening, and your family and other people close to you may have a difficult time adjusting as you go through the process.

For example, consider what happened to Peter, from Chapter 5, during the course of his therapy. Early in his sessions with Dr. Stone, he began acting, if anything, worse than he had before. He was just lucky, in fact, that his school was alerted about his therapy so that everyone there understood.

His behavior was worse at home, too. For a while it seemed as if the more his parents complained about his coming in late or about his misdeeds, the more he did them. That, of course, distressed his parents, as it would anyone's.

Shortly after this, though, he stopped being "bad." He got into fewer hassles at school, and when he was on the street it was to hang out, not to cause trouble. He even stopped seeing some of his old pals, because he realized they were pretty poor friends.

You would think this improvement would have made his parents happy, but it didn't. It scared them.

✦ ✦ ✦ ✦

It oftens happens in therapy that things get worse before they get better. People may feel worse as they grapple, sometimes without consciously realizing it, with emotions and memories that they've been avoiding. They may act worse as they test the insights they've gained. When Peter, for instance, first understood that he acted the way he did because of his home situation, he began, without realizing it, to test this idea. His behavior was really a way of asking how much of the trouble had really been his fault and how much his parents really cared about him. This was only the beginning, for when he uncovered all the hurt and rage he had buried, he acted out his feelings even more directly, and for a while things were pretty rugged.

Peter's parents' reaction to his eventual improvement isn't uncommon either. In fact, when you think about it, it makes sense. For much of his life they had assumed and responded to him as if he were "bad." The "new" Peter demanded changes in them, too, and that made them anxious. Frequently families learn to live with—and around—problems of individual members. When these problems are resolved and behavior changes, the whole family must adjust—and change is hard for everyone. Even Janet's parents, pleased as they were with her improvement, had to work at feeling comfortable with her new independence.

Parents may feel guilty, too, about their child's need for or interest in psychotherapy. It's easy to understand why people in Daniel's parents' situation—or even in the position of Theresa's mother—might feel guilty. Rightly or wrongly, they blamed themselves for their child's problem, as many parents do.

Finally, some parents resent the therapy or the therapist, seeing them as threats to their control over their children. If someone or some group outside the family begins to exert influence, a parent might understandably feel helpless and worried. And it sometimes happens that therapists, even ones who aren't doing much good for their young clients, become "good guys" in their patients' eyes, while parents are cast as the "bad guys." This can make life more complicated than it needs to be and provoke parents' hostility to the treatment.

INTERFERENCE

Parents who experience any or all of these negative feelings may take some kind of action. Even ones who were in favor of therapy at first may have second thoughts as their kids go through big changes. Parents may, for example, stop their child's therapy by forbidding it or by refusing to pay for it any longer. Or they may set up situations that make it difficult to continue: offer to send their child to camp, perhaps, or insist that he or she start a tutoring project or take an after-school job that conflicts with the therapy sessions. Parents have also been known to tell their child's therapist things like "Johnny doesn't really want to come anymore," while dropping hints to Johnny that maybe he *doesn't* want to come anymore—he no longer needs it, perhaps, or it isn't doing any good. Others have put a lot of pressure on the therapist to reveal details of what's been said and what's going on.

Sometimes, of course, parents are right in their concerns and complaints. They may not be able to afford therapy. They may feel that their child no longer needs treatment, or that a job, camp, or tutoring program would do him or her as much good. They may honestly feel that the therapist selected is not right for their child.

Whatever the reason for parents' "interference," it can be awkward, with the young patient caught in the middle. What should someone trapped in a situation like this do? The first step is to understand that it can happen and be prepared. Then he or she should do everything possible to get the true picture. Asking the following questions will help: "Are my parents really strapped for money, or are they unhappy about the changes in me?" "Am I really sure that I am, indeed, getting what I want out of therapy?" A good heart-to-heart with the interfering parents may also help. Hearing their child's feelings about his or her therapy may make parents feel better about letting it continue.

Perhaps the therapist could offer help and advice. Although a few adolescent therapists prefer to have nothing at all to do with their clients' families, most maintain some contact, and all should be willing to confer in cases where a report, some reassurance, or a discussion about the therapeutic status would help. After all, parents do have a right to know what is happening to their children—and talking over their child's problems with his or her therapist can be therapeutic in itself!

LIVING WITH THERAPY

What if the shoe is on the other foot? What if the teenager is living with a family member who is in therapy? Or what if *you* have a friend or relative who's undergoing some kind of psychiatric treatment? What do you do?

First, learn as much about the therapeutic process and the specific problems involved as you can. This book is a start. Others, listed on pages 130-132, should also help. Try talking with the person in therapy about his or her experiences; this can be good for both of you. And ask for information and advice from others who've been in similar situations as patient or bystander.

Check out your own attitudes. If you have in the back of your mind any of the negative ideas about therapy discussed in Chapter 2, these can make life hard for you and for your friend or relative. Do you think, for example, that turning to therapy is a sign of weakness? Remember, instead, that it takes strength to go for help. In any case, make sure any bad feelings you have about someone else's therapy aren't caused by popular stereotypes or old wives' tales.

Watch out for the green-eyed monster. Someone in therapy is often at the receiving end of a lot of other people's time and interest. If your sister is in therapy, for instance, it may seem to you that she is getting all your parents' attention. And, for the moment, maybe she is. Or you might naturally resent all the money being spent on your father's treatment—sure you want him to get better, but there are lots of things you hate to give up until then. Reactions like these can complicate the adjustment to another person's therapy. It may help to talk about them, openly, with someone else. Perhaps there are ways, too, of spending time alone with your parents, for example, or inexpensive treats you and your family can afford while budgets are tight. Try to develop more interests that don't require your family's participation. These may offset any feelings of "neglect" you have and may, in the long run, give you a healthy dose of independence.

Be prepared for change yourself. Anyone who is close to a person in therapy who is undergoing changes is going to feel a ripple effect. That person is likely, for instance, to relate to others in new and different ways. As a result, many families who "live with therapy" find it useful to get help for themselves as well. They may not need formal family therapy like the Fosters received, but some kind of guidance or counseling can often be worthwhile.

When things look especially bleak, it may lift your spirits to remember that whatever else may happen in therapy, when "successful" it is a process that provokes change and brings new insights. In the long run, everyone can benefit from that.

HAPPILY EVER AFTER?

Whatever *does* happen in therapy, at some point it is over. And when therapy is over, what then? First, it's important to understand what is meant by "over," and this in turn requires looking at why therapy was started in the first place.

Theresa, for example, went into treatment for some very specific problems. A few, like her headaches, she knew about. Others, like her difficulty in coping with the stresses in her life, she didn't. When those problems were resolved—when she no longer experienced the headaches and when she had come to understand why her current life was bumpy and had learned how to deal with those bumps—she was ready to stop seeing the psychologist.

When the Fosters realized that they were all getting along better, when Alec's behavior in school improved markedly, and when they all felt that they understood the conflicts that they had been living with, it seemed sensible to stop their sessions with Dr. Barclay, and she agreed.

Daniel's intensive treatment was over when his symptoms stopped, when he had a good grasp of what had happened to him, and when he and others felt he was ready to resume a "normal" life in the outside world.

✦ ✦ ✦ ✦

In each of these situations, there are two types of signals—outer and inner—that therapy should be ended. An "outer" sign is that troublesome symptoms ease: headaches disappear, behavior improves, tension relaxes, reality is understood. An "inner" sign is how the patient feels. Is she or he happier, calmer, less frightened? Does the person feel better about himself or herself? Does he or she have a good idea of how to cope with a similar problem independently in the future?

Outer signs are usually obvious, but sometimes they need to be pointed out. For example, Mrs. Kamm had to describe to Janet the changes she had observed in her, because Janet was afraid to admit them and have the therapy end. This is not unusual. Patients may be reluctant to let go of their therapist, feeling that their life has improved and it is all the therapist's doing. Of course, this isn't true! As you know by now, nothing can happen in any form of therapy without the patient's cooperation. Still, especially if someone feels nervous about leaving treatment (even if he or she didn't want to go in the first place), a therapist might recommend a gradual tapering off. Instead of sessions once a week, for instance, they might be held every two weeks, and then once a month, and then one or two more times later for a "checkup." That's what Peter did, even though the court didn't force him to. And Theresa stayed with the divorced-kids group for a long time —and for even longer with the friends she'd made there.

Although interpreting these "obvious" outer signals can be tricky, reading "inner" signals for clues about the appropriate time to end therapy can often be even more confusing. You would think, for instance, that someone who says, "I'm fine!" "I'm happy!" or "Finally I know what I'm doing" would no longer need treatment. But as mentioned before, people are not always the best judge of their own feelings, especially if they have been long buried or are intertwined with other feelings or problems. There often comes a point in therapy, for example, when patients want to stop because they are on the brink of confronting some important issue that they strongly want to avoid. Obviously, this is not the time to end therapy, though the patient may firmly disagree. Ideally, he or she will discuss things with the therapist—and, if possible, with family and with friends who've been in therapy—and take advice to continue treatment under serious consideration.

There are, of course, other ways that therapy might "end." Someone might simply decide not to go anymore. This is especially likely if he or she has been pressured into it. The same thing can be accomplished by going and simply not participating. Both actions, of course, are self-defeating and wasteful of the time that everyone invested while the patient was cooperating.

A therapist might end therapy, too, by saying there is "no point in continuing," or that circumstances no longer make it practical to meet. Therapy may also come to a screeching halt if parents interfere in one of the ways outlined in the previous chapter.

These kinds of involuntary termination are not the best, naturally, and might create some temporary confusion. But if a patient has devoted any amount of effort to the process at all, and if the therapist has been at all effective, treatment, however brief, will not have been wasted; something useful will surely have occurred, if only the introduction of the possibilities of self-awareness.

However therapy ends, it can be useful for the patient to spend time during those final sessions talking about specific problems that might come up. Having answers to questions like "What will I do if I get into the same kind of situation?" "What symp-

toms should I be on the lookout for—and then what
do I do?" and "Can I get in touch with you?" can
help reduce anxiety about "life after therapy."

MEASURING SUCCESS

Often people expect too much of therapy. Some
psychotherapists maintain that therapy is successful
in two-thirds of all cases, but of course that figure
cannot be scientifically proven. It would be nice if
we could all get a signed and sealed statement that
we were "cured" of whatever had been bothering
us. That would be proof, one might think, that therapy had "worked."

But in psychotherapy, a patient needs to look for
other, less clearly defined signs of success. One important measure is the difference between "then"
and "now." Take Janet, for example. Before therapy
her setups for failure had negative effects in all areas
of her life. Instead of the kinds of generally positive
experiences that encourage adolescent growth, she
was having negative ones that were closing off de-
velopment. The fact that with therapy things began
to go more smoothly than before—at school, at
home, and with friends—and that she came to feel
better about herself indicated that her treatment
had "worked."

"Happily ever after" exists only in fairy tales. Unfortunately, many people in this country have grown

up with the idea that "mental health" is a static, ideal condition. Naturally, they may be disappointed by the results of therapy. "Mental health," though, like physical health, implies the absence of disease, a sense of energy and well-being, and the ability to resist injury or infection, which in psychological terms are emotional scrapes and bruises.

Peter's therapy, for instance, will also be judged a success, though it won't change the world he lives in. His parents, his teachers, and the police will likely have lingering doubts about him, but he will finally be able to respond to them in noncombative ways. At first glance this may seem to be a minor achievement, but for Peter it may make the difference between leading a "normal" life and being an outcast.

NEW BEGINNING

Although it is true that therapy may "teach" much practical knowledge, such as the new behaviors the Fosters learned, its long-term benefits are far more important. It's useful, in fact, especially when a person is faced with the decision of whether to end therapy, to think of psychotherapy as a learning process that can last a lifetime without formal treatment —a new beginning of sorts rather than something that can be turned off and on like a faucet.

Of course, for someone like Daniel, therapy,

which might include medication, may be a long-term necessity. But most young people don't stay in therapy for long periods of time. Still, it is enough time for them to discover that they have found a resource, in addition to family and friends, that can be valuable in the future. Theresa may not return to Rachel or stick with the divorced-kids group for long; Janet will stop seeing Mrs. Kamm altogether. But not only will both therapists be available if needed; in addition, the girls have learned they can turn to someone like them for support, advice, and guidance whenever trouble strikes.

JUST ASK

HELPING ORGANIZATIONS OR SOCIAL-SERVICE DEPARTMENTS

For Advice About Legal Rights and Legal Restrictions

The American Civil Liberties Union
22 East 40th Street
New York, NY 10016
(Also, look in your phone directory for chapters in your area.)

Your local Legal Aid Society

Your state and local attorney general's office and department of health

For Advice About Specific Therapists' Credentials and Lists of Member Therapists

American Academy of Child Psychiatry
1424 16th Street, N.W.
Suite 201A
Washington, DC 20036

American Academy of Psychoanalysis
30 East 40th Street
Suite 608
New York, NY 10016

American Association for Marriage and Family Therapy
41 Central Park West
New York, NY 10023

American Orthopsychiatric Association
1775 Broadway
Suite 2501
New York, NY 10019

American Psychiatric Association
1700 18th Street, N.W.
Washington, DC 20009

American Psychoanalytic Association
1 East 57th Street
New York, NY 10022

American Psychological Association
1200 17th Street, N.W.
Washington, DC 20036

American Society for Adolescent Psychiatry
24 Green Valley Road
Wallingford, PA 19086

National Association of Social Workers
1425 H Street, N.W.
Suite 600
Washington, DC 20005

For Advice About Mental Health, Mental Illness, and Treatment

National Association for Mental Health
1800 North Kent Street
Rosslyn, VA 22209

The National Institute of Mental Health
5600 Fishers Lane
Rockville, MD 20852

Your community mental-health center

For Advice About or Sources for Free or Low-Cost Therapy

The child-welfare department or mental-health department
of your city, county, or state government

A local school of psychiatry, psychology, or social work

The psychiatric unit or adolescent unit of a local hospital

The social-service arm of your religion, such as
Catholic Charities

Jewish Board of Family Service
Protestant Welfare Board

Your local
  Community Service Society
  Children's Aid Society
  Family Service Association
  community center or neighborhood house
  YMCA or YWCA
  Salvation Army branch
  Mental Health Association

Also check the Yellow Pages under "Social Services" for other sources in your area, including hotlines that provide counseling and referrals for specific as well as general problems.

BOOKS

Nonfiction

(Some of these books were written for adults and some specifically for teens, but all are useful and informative for young adults.)

Bernheim, Kayla F., Richard R.J. Lewine, and Caroline T. Beale. *The Caring Family: Living with Chronic Mental Illness.* Random House, 1982.

> An adult book that discusses the problems faced by the families of the mentally ill.

Bush, Richard. *A Parent's Guide to Child Therapy.* Delacorte, 1980.

Summary of the various techniques used in therapy for young people.

Carlson, Dale. *Where's Your Head? Psychology for Teenagers.* Atheneum, 1977.

A well-written explanation of psychological concepts.

Erenberg, Miriam and Otto. *The Psychotherapy Maze.* Holt, 1977. Holt paper, 1977.

A clear guide to various forms of therapy.

Ewen, Robert. *Getting It Together: A Guide to Modern Psychological Analysis.* Watts, 1976.

A discussion for teens about neuroses and psychoanalysis.

Hall, Elizabeth. *Why We Do What We Do: A Look at Psychology.* Houghton Mifflin, 1973.

A discussion of psychological principles for young readers.

Herink, Richie, ed. *The Psychotherapy Handbook.* NAL paper, 1980.

Description of more than two hundred and fifty therapies.

Kiernan, Thomas. *Shrinks, Etc.: A Consumer's Guide to Psychotherapies.* Dial, 1974. Dell paper, 1976.

A catalog of possibilities.

Kovel, Joel. *A Complete Guide to Therapy: From Psychotherapy to Behavior Modification.* Pantheon, 1976.

In-depth discussions of the major forms of therapy.

LeShan, Eda. *In Search of Myself and Other Children.* Evans, 1976.

The author's description of her own psychotherapy.

————. *What's the Matter with Me?* Scholastic paper, 1974.

A book for young readers about emotional problems.

Marks, Jane. *Help: A Guide to Counseling and Therapy Without a Hassle.* Messner, 1976. Dell paper, 1979.

   A useful resource but references somewhat dated.

Mishara, Brian L., and Robert Patterson. *A Consumer's Guide to Mental Health: How to Find, Select, and Use Help.* Times Books, 1977. NAL paper, 1979.

   A summary of sources.

Ogg, Elizabeth. *The Psychotherapies Today.* Available for 50¢ from the Public Affairs Council, 381 Park Avenue South, New York, NY 10016.

Park, Clara Claiborne, and Leon N. Shapiro, M.D. *You Are Not Alone: Understanding and Dealing with Mental Illness.* Atlantic Monthly, 1976. Little, Brown paper, 1976.

   A dense but useful guide to the more serious forms of mental illness and their treatment.

Storr, Anthony. *The Art of Psychotherapy.* Simon & Schuster, 1980.

   A very well-written book, aimed at adults, by a therapist who explores and explains the therapeutic process.

Fiction

Anderson, Mary. *Step on a Crack.* Atheneum, 1978.

   A friend helps fifteen-year-old Sarah resolve her worries about her sanity.

Axline, Virginia M. *Dibs.* Houghton Mifflin, 1965. Ballantine paper, 1976.

   How therapy works for a disturbed boy.

Bauer, Marion D. *Tangled Butterfly.* Houghton Mifflin, 1980.

   A seventeen-year-old girl finds help from a former teacher when her family fails to acknowledge her emotional problems.

Coles, Robert, M.D. *Headsparks.* Little, Brown, 1975.

   Inside the head of a person under stress.

Green, Hannah. *I Never Promised You a Rose Garden.* Holt, 1964. NAL paper, 1977.

An account of the psychotherapy of a young woman.

Josephs, Rebecca. *Early Disorder.* Farrar, Straus & Giroux, 1980.

First-person account of a fifteen-year-old girl's slide into anorexia nervosa.

Meyer, Carolyn. *The Center: From a Troubled Past to a New Life.* Atheneum, 1979.

A troubled boy finds help and companionship by joining a group made up of other kids with problems.

Morganroth, Barbara. *Demons at My Door.* Atheneum, 1980.

An overachieving young woman tries hard to please everyone else and has a nervous breakdown as a result.

Neufeld, John. *Lisa, Bright and Dark.* Phillips, 1969. NAL paper, 1980.

Ripple effects from developing psychological problems.

Oneal, Zibby. *The Language of Goldfish.* Viking, 1980.

Carrie clings stubbornly to things of childhood and her past, creating an emotionally troubled passage to young adulthood.

Potter, Marian. *The Shared Room.* Morrow, 1979.

The impact on the family of a mentally ill parent.

Van Leeuwen, Jean. *Seems Like This Road Goes on Forever.* Dial, 1979.

Domineering, preoccupied parents cause a young woman to seek and find help from a psychologist.

Windsor, Patricia. *The Summer Before.* Harper & Row, 1973. Dell paper, 1974.

An account of the readjustment period following a bout with mental illness.

Wolitzer, Hilma. *Toby Lived Here*. Farrar, Straus & Giroux, 1978.

When Toby's widowed mother is placed in a state hospital following a nervous breakdown, Toby is swamped by fears and worries about her family's and her own future.

GLOSSARY

adolescence. Literally, "becoming adult"; the period—beginning about age eleven and continuing until about age twenty-one—during which a person grows to physical and social maturity.

conscious mind. The mental processes of which a person is aware.

crisis. In psychotherapeutic terms, (1) a turning point in one's life during which psychological support may be needed, or (2) the acute phase of a mental illness during which psychiatric help is required.

depression. A mental and emotional state characterized by feelings of worthlessness, despair, and lethargy among other symptoms; often disguised by overactivity or artificial "highs."

designated patient. In some forms of psychotherapy, a term used for the member of a group or family onto whom the problems of another or of the entire group are projected.

ego. In Freudian theory, the portion of personality that represents one's conscious image of oneself.

headshrinker or *shrink.* Slang terms for psychotherapist.

hypnotism. The creation of a state resembling sleep during which a trained practitioner, or hypnotist, can suggest behavior or probe blocked memories in the mind of a willing subject.

id. In Freudian theory, unconscious processes that represent a person's basic drives and urges.

identification. The unconscious imitation of some or all of another's personality.

insomnia. An inability to sleep.

neurosis. A pattern of behaviors, thoughts, and feelings that a person does not desire but over which the sufferer has no conscious control.

psyche. The mind and personality.

psychiatrist. A medical doctor who has had specialized training in the treatment of emotional, mental, and behavioral problems.

psychoanalyst or *analyst.* A psychotherapist who may or may not have some formal degree, but who does have training in Freudian or other techniques of in-depth analysis.

psychologist. A person with a Ph.D. degree (doctorate) in psychology who studies behavior and treats emotional, mental, and behavioral problems.

psychology. The study of behavior, mental processes, and emotional states.

psychosis. A mental or emotional state in which the disordered mind of the sufferer is unable to differentiate between reality and fantasy.

psychotherapist or *therapist.* A person who practices psychotherapy in some form.

psychotherapy. The treatment of emotional, mental, or behavioral problems or the exploration of personality by analysis, guided conversations, counseling, or other techniques.

resistance. A defensive process that is common in psychotherapy whereby the unconscious protects itself from painful probing by causing a patient to forget appointments or turn up late, fail to tell the therapist important information, or otherwise divert attention from the crucial matter at hand.

role-playing. In therapy, a technique in which a patient acts out conflicts or pretends to be someone else in order to understand painful situations or troublesome relationships better.

social worker. Someone with a master's degree in social work who after special training in psychology may serve as a psychotherapist.

superego. In Freudian theory, the portion of one's unconscious mind that functions as a conscience.

termination. In psychotherapy, the process of ending the relationship with a therapist or therapeutic group.

transference. A therapeutic process by which emotions or memories originally directed toward someone or something else of significance in a patient's life are focused on the therapist, enabling them to be worked through and resolved.

unconscious mind. Mental processes that occur without one's being aware of them.

INDEX

139

Residential treatment, 34, 39–
40, 104–112
cost of, 111–112
halfway houses and, 110, 111
for mental illness, 39–40, 111
Resistance to therapy, 70, 82
Rogerian therapy, 36
Rogers, Carl, 36
Role-playing, 38, 91–92

School records, confidentiality
of, 85–86
Self-help groups, 38–39, 46
Sexual overactivity, 54
Skinner, B. F., 37
Social-service agencies, 47, 72,
88, 129–130
Social workers, 40, 41–46, 72–
83, 101
certification of, 42
licensing of, 41–44
professional associations of,
43, 47, 129
training of, 41, 42
Stomachaches, 30, 58
Stress, 53, 58
mood and, 58
overreactions to, 54
success as, 12–13
symptoms of, 55–58
expressing, 59–60
Stress points, 59
Suicide-prevention bureaus, 107
Superego, 33

Tension, see Stress
Termination, see Ending therapy
Tests in therapy, 66–68
inaccuracies in, 68
objective, 68

subjective, 68
uses for, 67
Therapists
attitudes about names, 90
availability of, 74–76
certification of, 44–45, 48–49
choosing, 47–51
factors to look for, 48–50
questions to ask, 49, 50
confidentiality of, 26, 63, 64,
69, 89
cooperation with, 23
definition of, 24
finding, 47–51
first session with, 50, 74, 75,
89–90
as friends, 24–25, 70
as listeners, 25, 64–65
incompetent, 46–47
license for, 44, 48, 50
physical contact between patient and, 65
popular image of, 22, 25,
62
questions asked by, 25–26
relating to, 73–74, 75, 80
requirements for, 40–47
testing and, 66–68
trainee, 99–100
training of, 25, 40–47
types of, 40–47
Therapy
adolescent, 50, 80–81
arguments against, 19–23
beginnings of, 32–33
books about, 130–134
combination approaches, 38–
40
cost of, 22
definition of, 23